Project Rebirth

Project Rebirth:

Survival and the Strength of the Human Spirit from 9/11 Survivors

By Dr. Robin Stern
and Courtney E. Martin

DUTTON

DUTTON
Published by Penguin Group (USA) Inc.
375 Hudson Street, New York, New York 10014, U.S.A.
Penguin Group (Canada), 90 Eglinton Avenue East, Suite 700, Toronto, Ontario M4P 2Y3, Canada
(a division of Pearson Penguin Canada Inc.); Penguin Books Ltd, 80 Strand, London WC2R 0RL,
England; Penguin Ireland, 25 St Stephen's Green, Dublin 2, Ireland (a division of Penguin Books
Ltd); Penguin Group (Australia), 250 Camberwell Road, Camberwell, Victoria 3124, Australia
(a division of Pearson Australia Group Pty Ltd); Penguin Books India Pvt Ltd, 11 Community
Centre, Panchsheel Park, New Delhi—110 017, India; Penguin Group (NZ), 67 Apollo Drive,
Rosedale, North Shore 0632, New Zealand (a division of Pearson New Zealand Ltd); Penguin
Books (South Africa) (Pty) Ltd, 24 Sturdee Avenue, Rosebank, Johannesburg 2196, South Africa

Penguin Books Ltd, Registered Offices: 80 Strand, London WC2R 0RL, England

Published by Dutton, a member of Penguin Group (USA) Inc.

First printing, August 2011
10 9 8 7 6 5 4 3 2 1

REGISTERED TRADEMARK—MARCA REGISTRADA

LIBRARY OF CONGRESS CATALOGING-IN-PUBLICATION DATA
has been applied for.

ISBN 978-0-525-95226-8

Printed in the United States of America
Set in ITC Berkeley Oldstyle Std
Designed by Alissa Amell

We dedicate this book to all those who cared for the survivors of the tragedy on September 11, 2001, including the emergency workers, therapists, healers, educators, doctors, nurses, spiritual leaders, and, of course, their families and friends.

Their rebirth is in no small part your legacy as well.

Contents

Introduction

Construction workers in hard hats and steel-toed boots mill around the new shipment of steel, the steam from their coffee hanging in the early morning air around Ground Zero. A trailer door swings open and an architect walks out, rolled-up plans in one hand, iPhone in the other. He looks on as a group of workers weld giant metal skeletons together, sparks flying past ladders and giant spools of cable and tarps covering slats of wood.

This is what it looks like to physically rebuild after devastation.

But what does it look like to emotionally and spiritually rebuild? This was the question that preoccupied us—a journalist and a psychoanalyst—as we mined the lives of those who had been directly affected by the tragic events of September 11, 2001. We wanted to understand how ordinary people recover from grief, dust off the ashes of devastation, make sense of injustice and just plain bad luck, and emerge new, different, maybe even more whole.

We were not aiming for pat lessons. Too much has already been written that tries to reduce what happened on that fateful day into feel-good sound bites, political propaganda, or ratings-hyping melodrama. September 11th, like every historic moment, has been shaped and shifted, prodded and poked, adopted and adapted for various purposes over the past ten years. Most often, this work has been done with good intentions, but too much of the time, the true depth of the physical, emotional, and sometimes spiritual transformations that were rooted in that day's tragic events were lost.

There are such layers to the story of September 11th and its survivors, such nuances, such paradox. There is heroism and cowardice, nurturance and violence, anger and love—the whole panoply of human emotions circulating around this one day of unimaginable loss. Only that greatest and most difficult teacher of all, time, could really offer us the insights that we needed to do justice to these eight stories. It has now been ten full years since we first saw that indelible image of a Boeing 757 crashing into the North Tower of the World Trade Center, unbelievable as that is.

In those ten years, so much has happened. Technologically, culturally, and politically, we live in a truly new world—one where disasters often play out online before anyone thinks to turn on a television, as they did on September 11th. There are cottage industries and whole branches of the government devoted to fighting the kind of threat we faced on September 11th. Even our language is different—"terrorism" has become a household word, something that could slip off the tongue of any ten-year-old in this nation. We watch revolutions and natural disasters play out on Twitter and send donations via text message—all of which would have been inconceivable in the fateful fall of 2001.

But this book is not about technological or cultural shifts, nor is it about the analysis of national security advisers or international development experts. This book is not about politics or media or even the controversy that has surrounded the revisioning of Ground Zero or the creation of the September 11th Museum. This book is about the expertise and experiences of regular people. It is about Nick, Brian, Charles, Larry, Tim, Joe, Debbie, and Tanya—eight studies in grief and resilience, loss and progress, sadness and transformation.

These lessons, after all, are most commonly culled from extraordinary circumstances, but their roots are universal. We all lose. We all grieve. We are all compelled to recover. For most of us, this experience occurs as part of life's natural, but inevitable, sadness— a mother passing away from breast cancer, a life partner breaking one's heart by leaving for someone else, a friend struck by a heart attack despite seeming healthy. Though these circumstances are statistically ordinary, they are no less than deeply painful, leaving us grappling for wisdom and hope amid the sudden sense of foreign and consuming darkness.

But the extraordinary, too, is becoming more ordinary. Sudden disasters, like the one that struck America on September 11, 2001, are increasingly common because of global terrorism and climate change. "Where were you the day Kennedy was assassinated?" has become "Where were you the day the earthquake devastated Haiti? Where were you the day Katrina decimated New Orleans? Where were you when the World Trade towers and the Pentagon were hit?" In our increasingly insecure world, we are all subject to disaster and the collective project of reconstituting our communities, not to mention our worldview, afterward.

We were both in New York on September 11th. Robin, who has had her own psychoanalytic practice for thirty years, was on her way to see some patients that morning (eventually, she would counsel many clients directly affected by September 11th). Courtney was still asleep in her Barnard College dorm when the first plane hit the towers.

Robin's first thoughts, upon finding out about the terrorist attacks, were of her two children, Scott and Melissa, and her husband, Frank. *Were they safe? How could she immediately get to them?* Courtney's first thoughts were also of her family—her parents so far away in Colorado Springs, her brother even farther in San Francisco. These questions quickly migrated to the future. *What did this all mean about her senior year, her future beyond college, the country's future?*

Robin's family and Courtney's dreams were safe, although forever changed by that horrible day. In the years that followed, we would become writing partners, but more than that, dear friends. When *Project Rebirth* came about, we jumped at the chance to work together, especially with such historic and profound stories as those found in this book. Courtney brings her journalistic training to the page, and Robin brings her vast experience as a clinician to help to present the grieving process in a new way. We both strongly believe that stories are tools of transformation—Courtney's usually live on the page and Robin's, more often, in the safe haven of her clinical practice—and that is also why the format of this book was so appealing to us.

In this book, we have brought both of our sensibilities and areas of expertise to bear, and we hope it makes for an approachable, layered, and inspiring read. Having the opportunity to delve into these stories, discuss them over countless lunches and coffees, laugh and cry together, and ask the subjects, ourselves, and each other so many big questions has been a gift of indescribable proportions. We hope the reverence we have for these people's lives is reflected in the book that you are about to experience.

As explained above, this book is not about politics. This book is about the personal. It is about the lives—logistical, emotional, unique, and inspiring—that are shattered by moments like 8:46 A.M., September 11, 2001, and then put back together during the years that followed. It is also not a book about psychology, per se. Though Robin is a psychoanalyst by training, she's more committed to practical lessons than abstract theory. Theory isn't supple and nuanced enough, in our view, to truly wrap itself around the breadth and depth of these stories. As sociologist Kai T. Erikson wrote of survivors whom he profiled, "People like that have been the victims of so many different forces outside their control that one hesitates to imprison them again between the cold parentheses of a theory."

Instead, we listened to the testimony of these survivors, letting them be the real authorities on their own grieving and healing processes. We have applied psychological insights when it seemed necessary and translated them for the layperson, more out of an instinct to share ideas than an attempt to justify what is evident: Human beings are both undeniably fragile *and* astoundingly resilient.

Grief, like any other emotional process, is as unique as a fingerprint. In the pages that follow, you will get a sense of where the contemporary thinking is on grief, having moved away from old ideas. One of the things that we were so struck by as we immersed ourselves in these stories—researching, interviewing, writing, discussing, revising, and most important, listening to the voices and stories of 9/11 survivors—was that the public dialogue on loss has been severely limited. If you ask the average person what they know about grief, they will usually throw out the phrase "stages of grief." Either knowingly or not, many of us reference the influential theory of Elisabeth Kübler-Ross, in which she posited that there were five distinct stages of grief that each person must go through. But the latest research on loss proves that Kübler-Ross's once ground-breaking theory was inadequate to describe the full range of grief reactions. The average person's journey through grief is far less uniform— more like a roller coaster than a ski lift.

Sigmund Freud, the father of psychoanalysis, made his own

lasting impression on the public psyche when it comes to loss. Freud posited his foundational theory of grieving in his 1917 essay, "Mourning and Melancholia," in which he attempted to distinguish between healthy grieving and melancholia, a state of ongoing depression. He argued that one must do "mourning work," responding to the "call of reality" until she can "renounce the object by declaring its death" (the object being the lost loved one). The melancholic mourner, in contrast, becomes destructively attached to a lost loved one, unable to "kill" him or her off in one's own mind.

As you'll see in the coming pages, the individuals who lost loved ones in the attacks of September 11th, did not so much work through their grief—suggesting a finite amount of sadness, eventually depleted to nothing—as open up to it, acknowledge it, integrate it. No mourner chose to cease thinking about their beloved, so much as shift the nature of the relationship—from in the flesh to in the mind and heart. A mother, lost, is no longer a source of home-made soup and a good, long dinner conversation, but she still influences her son in a daily, sacred way. A fiancé, dead so young and suddenly, can no longer caress the bare shoulder of his love, but the memory of his tenderness can still make her feel loved.

We know, then, what grief is not—direct, contained, predictable. What it *is*, well, that's still being explored by some of psychology's finest thinkers and researchers. In this book, you will see the grief process wax and wane in the lives of real, relatable people. This storied approach is critical, as the science around grief continues to tie itself up in knots about how to describe the widely variant types of sadness that affect the grieving human. Dr. Kathy Shear of Columbia University describes the emotional experience of grief as akin to the physical experience of inflammation: "We don't think of natural grief as an illness, primarily because there's so much baggage associated with illness. But some very prominent thinkers and researchers have, in fact, said that we should consider grief similar to inflammation, a natural healing response to injury." In this case, of course, the injury is the loss, and one's emotional defenses, like the immune system, rise up to process and heal the psyche.

Joan Didion, acclaimed memoirist, took great comfort in a different metaphor for grief's all-consuming hold on a widow's consciousness: waves. In her engrossing account of her husband's death and what came after, *The Year of Magical Thinking*, she references Dr. Michael Lindemann's work. The chief of psychiatry at Massachusetts General Hospital, he defines grief as "sensations of somatic distress occurring in waves lasting from twenty minutes to an hour at a time."

Dr. George Bonanno, also of Columbia University, has studied grief and trauma over two decades and in a variety of contexts, many of them with parallels to September 11th. He believes that waves like the ones Lindemann describes are an accurate depiction of a state that comes and goes, rather than sticking around in some unceasing, uniform way. Additionally, he argues that there are four potential trajectories of grief: "resilience, recovery, chronic dysfunction, and delayed grief or trauma."

The notion of "delayed grief" is a highly contested one. Some well-respected experts in the field, Shear among the most vocal, have argued that about 10 percent of bereaved people experience *complicated grief*, marked by the presence of prolonged feelings of disbelief and anger, a sense of emptiness, suicidal thoughts, and estrangement from other people. In fact, according to the *Canadian Medical Association Journal*, the next edition of the *Diagnostic and Statistical Manual of Mental Disorders*—the DSM-5, scheduled for publication in 2013—is likely to contain a new entry called "bereavement-related disorder," which will attempt to describe and classify grief that goes on and on.

Dr. Leeat Granek, a Toronto-based psychologist, worries that such an inclusion pathologizes grief, rather than seeing it as a normal part of the human experience: "Many of the mental illnesses in the DSM are social constructions that are based on the cultural zeitgeist at the moment. We already live in a culture that is intolerant of grief and loss in general. The message is often, 'You need to move on, you need to see someone.'" Granek is leading a bourgeoning movement advocating for the reconceptualization of grief, particularly in the North American context, where is has been misunderstood and neglected for too long. The cultural context within which grief emerges is key in understanding how we process. The brave eight who are featured in this book all mourned their losses in the United States, but each has very particular cultural scripts within that commonality.

Understanding grief, in all its manifestations and cultural mores, is not just beneficial for our own inevitable experiences of loss, but so that we might support others through theirs. Megan O'Rourke reflected on her grief process following her own mother's death in a series for Slate.com, which evolved into her book, *The Long Goodbye*. She explains, "I am not surprised to find that it is a lonely life: After all, the person who brought me into the world is gone. But it is more than that. I feel not just that I am, but that the world around me is deeply unprepared to deal with grief."

She goes on to detail the well-intentioned yet unsatisfying emails that she got from friends and colleagues following her mother's death. They echoed one another, sympathetic, yet inadequate: "At least she's no longer suffering." O'Rourke was crushed by the lack of wise support. She is not alone. So many of us have felt abandoned during times of great suffering, left to the fumbling condolences of a world that is both uninformed about grief and also afraid of what it indicates: that we all love and lose, that we all will die. It's imperative that we become more aware of the complex truths about grief, and in turn, more skillful in comforting one another, so that we, too, may one day receive the same substantial support in return.

This is also not just a book about grief. It is, first and foremost, a book about resilience. It is about that miraculous process by which people whose lives have been shattered in an instant, manage to find the strength to pick up the pieces and put them back together again—not in the same way as before, but in a new, reintegrated form.

Resilience is often assumed to be a personality trait, something you are either lucky to be born with, or doomed to be born without, but it is actually more accurately thought of as a process. A resilient person essentially draws on inner resources and calls on community support in order to move forward after disappointment, failure, or trauma. Research confirms that the presence of resilience is encouraged or discouraged by the communities and environments of which we find ourselves a part. When difficult things happen to us—divorce, illness, death, job loss, etc.—we are able to weather those changes based on a unique combination of our own hard-wiring and psychological resources in consort with the protective factors that our families and communities, social policies, and schools create for us.

Resilience has been a widely discussed topic as of late, identified by educators, mental health professionals, and researchers as one of the key ingredients to living a long, happy life. Bonanno, among others, has found that resilience, rather than some rarified quality, is actually quite common, and that there are "multiple, unexpected pathways" to get there. In fact, resilience researchers warn, what might sometimes look like a short-term decline in mental health can actually be a sign of the human psyche rallying its resources for ultimate recovery.

Hardship does have the capacity to make us hardier. A recent study in *The Journal of Personality and Social Psychology*, for example, found that some of those who have experienced multiple stressful events in life become more robust—picking themselves up and integrating their lessons faster than those who haven't experienced many losses or life changes. Resilience, it turns out, can be like a muscle, growing stronger with use.

Another recent study, this one aptly titled "That Which Doesn't

Kill Us Can Make Us Stronger (and More Satisfied with Life)" and appearing in the journal *Psychology & Health*, found that identifying oneself as a "survivor" is actually positively correlated with life satisfaction. In other words, those who have been through hell and made it out feel like life is a bit more heavenly than those who never have to struggle through such darkness.

In this book, we look at the ways in which these resilient people took their grief and remolded it, bringing new meaning into their lives. They mourned, and continue to do so in various ways, but also carried on as an affirmation of life's preciousness and the heart's capacity for renewal.

But they didn't do it alone. So often, the eight survivors featured in this book were and still are deeply supported by caring communities—both informal and formal. Their families, friends, and extended networks stand as testament to the healing power of simple and profound presence and love. One hand held after the next, one hug given and received after the next, one sad or angry sentiment articulated and heard after the next. In Bishop Stephen Paul Bouman's moving book, *Grace All Around Us: Embracing God's Promise in Tragedy and Loss*, he relays relying on the powerful wisdom of a South African bishop post-9/11: "In our culture, when tragedy happens, we don't all visit at once. We come a few at a time so that each time the person in sorrow has to answer the door and tell the story again of what happened and shed the tears. As the story is told again and again, healing can begin."

The survivors' caregivers, therapists, support groups, and spiritual mentors also show up in these pages—people whose commitment to their work and engagement with the people they care for is deeply moving, particularly in the face of such destruction. Disaster, as a subject, has been around, at least in the American context, since we first took stock of what was lost—so many lives, rigid social roles, a sense of abundance—following World War II. The idea of disaster mental health, more specifically, was first put on the conceptual map with Erikson's 1976 book, *Everything in Its Path: Destruction of Community in the Buffalo Creek Flood*, in which he asked, "What is 'disaster,' anyway?" and then answered in a way that reads as eerily prescient when considering our subject, an event that wouldn't take place for twenty-five years yet: "a sharp and furious eruption of some kind that splinters the silence for one terrible moment and then goes away." Erikson, like us, centered the voices of the victims of that tragedy, arguing that they deserved a more researched and skilled response from professionals in the mental health field.

Great caregivers, psychologists, sociologists, and the like have heeded his call ever since, creating institutes, field guides, journals, and coalitions in order to constantly perfect our capacity to respond in moments of crisis to those who need it most. As Laura van Dernoot Lipsky, author of *Trauma Stewardship: An Everyday Guide to Caring for Self While Caring for Others*, writes, "Many of us who do frontline work to ease trauma and bring about social and environmental change understand that bearing witness, amplifying the story, and taking right action are our most important tasks. But how do we witness, and what is right action?" These questions, like all of the wisest inquiries, are unanswerable, to some extent. And yet, those whose life work is located in the trenches of human suffering continue to explore ever more skillful ways of helping healing along.

It's not just about the individual professional's capacity, of course, but also about the capacity to coordinate a response among professionals working in a variety of realms. An unprecedented partnership was forged following September 11th between two very different organizations: Disaster Psychiatry Outreach and New York Disaster Interfaith Services. They were able to work together to acknowledge that healing the whole victim is not just about emotion, nor is it just about spirit, but about the combination of the two.

In a critical, co-edited new book, *Creating Spiritual and Psychological Resilience: Integrating Care in Disaster Relief Work*, Grant H. Brenner, Daniel H. Bush, and Joshua Moses write: "These partnerships have the potential to help societies harness the transformational capacities disasters hold for resilience—for how we might redress chronic, long-simmering ills in new ways, comfort the bereaved, rebuild with the survivors, and perhaps even help people better situations they were in prior to disasters." Indeed, Dr. April Naturale, who directed the disaster mental health response called Project Liberty, found that many of the people her organization served reported that they never would have sought mental health services prior to September 11th, but felt that the experience had deeply enriched their lives in many different areas.

Project Rebirth is ultimately a book about the power of the human spirit to rebuild itself—within *and* among community. Those who lost loved ones in the World Trade towers or barely escaped from the wreckage themselves had their lives instantaneously devastated. Who they were on September 10, 2001—how they spent each day, how they saw the world, what they expected from the future—was entirely dismantled. They were put in the unenviable position of reconstructing their very lives. And therein lies the miracle. They did it. They took the most malicious misfortune imaginable and transformed it—tear by tear, day by day, dawn by dawn.

They are not alone. It wasn't just those directly affected by the events of September 11 who felt their lives forever change. We all got a taste of destabilization. Further still, even if in a drastically different context, we all mourn. We hope that in these courageous stories you will find echoes of your own experiences of loss and recovery. We hope that this book will serve as comfort amid discomfort, these words as reconnection to hope, these flawed and fierce examples as a reminder of the universal human capacity for resilience.

In a world in which so many of our days are filled with the minutiae of existence—the cable bill, the carpool schedule, the bureaucracy at work, at school, at the doctor's office—it's more important than ever that we take a moment to focus on the most essential elements of our existence. At a time when 140 characters and thirty-second sound bites have become our dominant forms of communication, this book offers the depth that comes from decade-long stories and painstaking reflection.

Tragedy like the kind faced by the people profiled in this book forces that quality of focus. It inspires us to ask the most basic questions that we face as human beings: What is my life about? What's important? How can I use my energy for good? Have I loved well? What is my legacy? What's more, it compels us to not settle for the easy answers. Instead, we honor the complexity of our lives and losses by stepping away from the cacophony of modern life and really listening to the wisdom in these long-developing stories.

If these survivors' struggles teach us anything, it is that we all have an opportunity to ask these questions of ourselves on a regular basis. Trauma and loss may be our most profound motivators, but we don't need to wait on them to start seeking out our true path or valuing the people we love.

Ultimately, the biggest tribute to the survivors featured in this book is not the anniversary ceremonies that occur each September 11, beautiful as they may be. It's not feeling sorry for them or dramatizing their very real loss. The ultimate tribute to the survivors of September 11, 2001, is bearing witness to the stories of their recovery, and incorporating some of their wisdom into our own lives—today. It is recognizing how wildly precious and fleeting our lives are, that we have no other viable choice, really, but to make them as courageous and loving as possible.

A Note on Project Rebirth

Just as there are stories *within* this book, there is a story *of* this book.

It all begins, interestingly enough, in Hollywood. Jim Whitaker, a filmmaker, lost his beloved mother in the spring of 2001. One of five brothers, he watched with great intrigue and no small amount of sadness as his siblings all processed his mother's death differently.

Following the World Trade Center attacks, Jim saw even more evidence of how grief and resilience manifest in so many different forms, and realized that he was being offered a historic opportunity to document its variable unfolding. So Whitaker and his filmmaking team, including director of photography, Thomas Lappin, set up 35-millimeter motion-picture time-lapse cameras throughout the Ground Zero site to document the physical rebuilding and, along with a talented team of producers, found a small but diverse group of people who had been directly affected by the terrorist attacks of September 11 and set about earning their trust. He interviewed them each year on the anniversary of the attacks and used their words as the basis for a powerful documentary film.

Over the years, Project Rebirth—as it would come to be known—grew and grew. The filming of the physical site now constitutes the largest time-lapse project in human history. The challenges and opportunities involved in documenting the rebuilding of the human spirit appealed to educators, museum curators, philanthropists, and artists alike. Soon it became clear that a book created out of the rare and rich footage would be both a wonderful complement to the film and a worthwhile resource all on its own.

The film premiered at the Sundance Film Festival to great critical acclaim in January of 2011 and was subsequently released in theaters in August, by Oscilloscope Laboratories, and will be shown on Showtime in September. The film, as well as other original programming created by the team that worked on it, will eventually be housed at the National September 11 Memorial & Museum located at Ground Zero.

The film, it should be noted, features only five of the original subjects. The book captures the recovery of eight of those people who dedicated themselves for the duration of the filming process. We are proud that it allows the stories of these individuals—both those featured in the film and those whose stories did not make it onto celluloid—to be fleshed out, filled in, and mined for even more instructive and inspirational moments from the front lines of resilience.

Rather than summarizing the film, the book serves as a completely new lens through which to see the courage that followed the tragedy of September 11th. We all drew from the same unprecedented source material—hours and hours of interviews—but emerged with different creations. In this way, the entire project is also a powerful study in collaboration and historicization. In pursuit of the many truths about tragedy and the survival of the human spirit, we have also discovered how many ways there are to look at the same powerful human story.

Finally, readers should know that a portion of the proceeds from the book will be donated to the subjects herein, September 11th–related organizations of their choosing, as well as the Project Rebirth Center, to develop and provide new multimedia tools to aid the therapists, academics, first responders, and others working with people dealing with grief.

A Little Bird Told Me

Nick Chirls

N ick Chirls sits down at his desk and powers up his computer. As his hand manipulates the mouse to scroll through the plummeting stock prices of 2008, he imagines his mother's hand doing the same. A co-worker stops by his cubicle to share a story, and as he chuckles, he imagines his mother's laugh reverberating off the windowed walls. As he sips his coffee at midmorning, starting to fade as his late night with friends finally catches up with him, he imagines his mother sipping her coffee as she tried to get through another long workday.

This is how Nick stays connected to his mother—though she has been dead for seven years now. It is through the daily, sometimes mundane tasks and interactions of a Wall Street trader that he feels her presence. The morning meetings. The elevator banter. The office chairs. Most people would consider it odd for a kid to seek out a maternal presence in the masculine hubbub of a finance firm, but for Nick, it makes perfect sense. He explains, "I feel like I'm doing something that she absolutely would have wanted me to do . . . something that will continue her work, her legacy."

. . .

Before Nick had ever weighed the heavy nature of legacy, before he'd ever heard of Al-Qaeda or Osama bin Laden, before his mom ever took a job with Cantor Fitzgerald on the 104th floor of One World Trade Center, the Chirls were a happy, seemingly conventional family living in Princeton, New Jersey. Nick, the eldest of three, loved to help his mom clear the dishes and talk to her about everything under the sun—financial markets, politics, girls. Unlike a lot of his friends, aching through the rebellions of adolescence, he had a genuine friendship with his mother, a real respect for her bright mind: "She had a view on everything and she would say anything."

Whenever Nick confronted obstacles—whether it was on the squash court, in the classroom where he faced mountains of homework at his rigorous high school, or in his buzzing social life—he would go to his mom for guidance. Nick remembers a particular exchange that stuck with him:

My mom and I were talking and I came up with the question, "Why try?" I was frustrated over something and I just wanted to say, "Forget it. I don't feel like doing it. Who really cares about this one thing, or anything really?" And she said something that I'll never forget: "We try to open doors for ourselves. It's not a matter of what's going to come of it. It's a matter of giving yourself options." That had an incredible impact on me. I try not to limit myself.

Indeed, Catherine Ellen Chirls refused to accept conventional limitations. She was devoted to her family—always spearheading adventures and rich dinner table conversations, organizing raucous birthday celebrations, and even filming them with her state-of-the-art camcorder—but she was also a dedicated career woman. At home, she was the warm center of the Chirls's universe, the sun around which the three kids—Dylan, Sydney, and Nick—and her loving husband, David, orbited. At work, she was known for being tough and brazen and for maintaining an eye-on-the-prize mentality at all times. Though the juggle of home and work must have been stressful, Nick remembers only the sheer passion that his mother exuded about both her family and her portfolio. "Wall Street, she enjoyed," he remembers. "Her family, she loved."

Which is partly why Catherine and David decided in early 2001 that it was time for the family to move from their beloved home in Brooklyn Heights to Princeton. They figured that by moving to the suburbs, the kids could spread out a little more, and Nick could go to a top-notch high school—the kind that would inevitably open the doors Catherine had referenced. City living was a cacophonous joy, but it was time to slow down a little, get some space, make life a little easier.

Nick was not happy about moving. All of his friends were in Brooklyn Heights, everyone he had ever known and loved, plus his favorite spots—Grimaldi's, Hot Bagels, the promenade, with its cobblestones and breathtaking view of Lower Manhattan. These people, these places, made up his small, happy world, and he didn't want to disrupt that. He couldn't figure out why his parents insisted on moving to a state that was the consistent butt of New Yorkers' jokes.

But when you're fifteen, of course, your opinion counts only so much. Eventually, he packed up his little room like everyone else in the family and headed across the Hudson to his new home. The only consolation was that he got a new dog and named it . . . what else? Brooklyn.

• • •

Nick was in the library, doing some research for an assignment, when static signaling an impending announcement crackled from the intercom. *All students. All faculty. Don't go to your next class. Meet in the assembly hall in fifteen minutes.*

He shuffled to the assembly hall like everyone else, numbly letting the river of students take him to their collective destination. The worried buzz washed over him. He stood in the back, wondering what all the fuss was about. The headmaster stood before the student body and informed them that an airplane had flown into the World Trade Center. Nick's stomach dropped. He went instantaneously numb. His legs were shaking. He explains, "I went through my whole life thinking nothing could ever happen to me. Even at that point I thought, *My mom can't be dead.*"

But then the headmaster said something that fractured his numbness: "Our nation is under attack."

The words were so definitive, so grave. Nick suddenly felt ill. He didn't want to be here, among all of these concerned strangers, these anonymous faces who had no idea who he was, who his mother was, the danger she was in. He slipped outside, slumped onto a nearby bench, and started crying.

If Nick had been back at Hunter College High, his old school, he would have been surrounded by friends who not only knew his mom had just taken a job in the World Trade Center, but knew what her chocolate chip cookies tasted like, knew how her voice traveled up flights of stairs with ease, knew how much he depended on her for wisdom and comfort. In Princeton, he knew almost no one, and those he had met in his one week at the Lawrenceville School certainly had no idea that his mother was potentially scared, hurt, or, the unthinkable, dead. Nick had never felt so alone.

He launched into problem-solving mode. *What floor did his mother say she worked on again?* He racked his brain for the number. *What did she last say to him when she left this morning? Was it "I love you"? Where was she right at this very moment? Was she scared? Had she called his dad? How could he get to her?*

As a dozen unanswerable questions raced through his brain, his squash coach wandered over and sat next to him. "Do you want to use my cell phone to try to call her?" he asked.

Nick grabbed the cell with great relief. At least one person knew him well enough to know that this was not just a weird morning, but a personal crisis. Nick and his parents had met the squash coach before he even started at Lawrenceville. The coach knew that his mom worked in the financial industry.

Nick dialed his mom's number, but her voice mail immediately picked up. "No answer," he said, looking up at his coach through his tears.

"Let me give you a ride home."

When Nick got there, home had already gone from being the usual boisterous place to a place of tense limbo. Nick's longtime housekeeper cried, devastated that her employer and friend was suddenly missing. His little brother and sister were weepy and confused. His dad was already in the car trying to get to New York.

As the news crept in, hope slipped out. Catherine worked on the 104th floor, right above the impact of the plane. If she, by some miracle, survived the explosion that the plane created, there was little hope that she could have gotten out of the tower—the elevators and staircases had most likely been destroyed. There was no news from other Cantor Fitzgerald employees. Reportedly, hospital staff in downtown Manhattan waited for injured survivors that, largely, never showed up. It was evident rather quickly that if you were in the World Trade Center on September 11, 2001, you most likely escaped uninjured or perished.

Nick's father returned, unable to get to Manhattan. The kids went for a swim in their backyard pool, just to do something, then sort of drifted in and out of rooms like zombies. Nick and his father tried to explain the situation in the least frightening terms possible to six-year-old Dylan and ten-year-old Sydney, but there really was no way to make it less awful. As night fell, they all settled into David and Catherine's big bed together to try to make it through the night. Their first night without her.

. . .

On September 22, 2001, Nick climbed the steps to the podium to deliver his mother's eulogy. He looked out at the sea of grieving faces belonging to his mother's friends and old colleagues, extended family and old roommates. Some people, he realized, he'd never even set eyes on before. All of these sad women and men—some of them familiar, some of them strangers—had been touched by his mother.

He was not surprised there were so many of them. His mother had lived that kind of life—making friends wherever she went. "She loved life more than anyone I knew. She just loved living," Nick explained. What did surprise him was how lonely he felt even in the midst of so much community. The whole concept of a funeral felt strange, like an ill-fitting suit, formal and performative. But he knew it would be important to his mom that he speak, and he wanted to continue to honor her.

He stood before the crowd, cleared his throat, and began:

My mom was remarkable. She was so enthusiastic about everything she did. She always had her own individual views and sense of reason. She was a great daughter, a fantastic sister, a wonderful wife, and most importantly, she was an amazing mother.

Just as Nick finished this sentence, a baby sparrow, as tiny as a plum, landed on his head. The audience collectively gasped. "It landed so gently," he remembers, "that I thought it was a piece of paper or something. It didn't fly into my head. It very deliberately landed there. It wasn't *almost* perfect. It was perfect."

When Nick reached up to figure out what it was, the sparrow allowed him to pick it up and hold it in his hand. He looked into its tiny black eyes for a moment and, as impossible as it sounds, felt his mom stare back. He remembers, "I could swear to God there was some sort of recognition. It looked at me and then it flew away."

Nick is not a religious person or someone interested in new age theories. He's never believed in reincarnation or even some sort of thin veil between life and death. Even at the kind of moments when most people look to some sort of faith or philosophy to comfort them, to assure them that their loved one is in a better place, Nick does not. He likes facts—measurable and clear. He's comforted most by straight talk.

But despite Nick's lack of belief in God or a greater force in the universe, he remains convinced that what he experienced that day was supernatural. "There is no doubt in my mind that my mom was there and that there was something incredibly spiritual about it," Nick says. "It can't be explained."

The experience of loss, like Nick's, like anyone's, really, is one of profound ineffability. We create stories around these experiences so that we can understand them better, but in truth, death often puts people face-to-face with the inexplicable nature of life, death, and love. Nick explored this later in his eulogy for his mom:

So what will I do now without her? I'll be fine. She has given me enough so that I will be able to get through this, and that is what determines a great mother. In a weird way, I feel she has prepared me for all of this.

In a sense, the visitation of the sparrow was one more form of preparation. Nick's experience that day transcended all of his comfortable habits of mind. Even Nick, whose bourgeoning worldview was thrown off kilter by this spiritual experience, recognizes it as a gift: "It was beautiful. I'm incredibly glad that it happened. I really didn't have any faith that she was anywhere before that. Afterwards, I think I did. I think she's somewhere."

Somewhere. This is the province of grieving as people struggle to imagine where it is that their loved one has gone. Bonanno, author of *The Other Side of Sadness*, writes, "Death pulls at the veil of mundane life and, at least temporarily, exposes us to a universe of questions, many of which have no clear answer." Such was the case for Nick. In fact, his mom's death led him down a long, sometimes treacherous path of questioning—questioning his country, his friends, his family, and, most affecting of all, his future.

. . .

In the years following September 11, Nick understandably struggled. His English teacher, who had also lost his mom as a teenager, talked openly about how difficult it was to process and how much writing had served as his outlet in the midst of mourning. Nick took his advice to heart. After everyone else in the house had gone to bed, he would often start to write—letting the words flow out of him in a way that tears never seemed to. "Business and math are still my biggest interests," Nick explains, shortly after losing his mom. "But that's not all there is. I find great comfort in writing."

Comfort had become a sparse commodity after his mom's death. Nick was accustomed to looking to his mom for comfort, but thoughts of her actually provoked pain now; every time he thought of her, it was as if he were a small child, reaching for a security blanket, only to be pricked by a splinter woven through its shabby threads.

In December of 2001, Nick, his father, and his two siblings moved back to Brooklyn Heights, surrounded, once again, by all the familiar haunts. And yet, nothing felt the same. Not only was his mom no longer there to welcome him home or ask him about his day, but his entire family composition was changing. Nick's father,

David, started dating one of Nick's mother's good friends, Bobbi. They would go on to marry in April of 2003.

Nick found comfort in other places—namely, global financial services firm Cantor Fitzgerald, where he got a highly competitive internship when he was just seventeen years old.

Cantor Fitzgerald, whose corporate headquarters were unluckily located on floors 101 through 105 of One World Trade Center, right above the impact zone, lost 658 employees in the attacks on September 11, Nick's mom among them. That was two-thirds of their workforce at the time and substantially more than the proportion of employees lost by any of the other businesses in the World Trade Center, or even the police or fire departments.

From the moment Nick started interviewing with Cantor, he felt like he had found his people: "Everyone there either lost someone close to them or works next to someone who lost someone close to them. Everyone was affected."

Being surrounded by people who had also been directly affected by September 11th was a real relief for Nick. While the thirty students who lost a parent at nearby private school, Dalton, for example, had one another to lean on, Nick didn't have a lot of close friends who were also in mourning. At Cantor, he not only learned about every facet of financial services, but felt surrounded by people who understood his loss, and—in a sense—reunited him with his mom. In 2003, he explains, "Every day I worked there, I thought about my mom. I love it there."

"In five years, I don't want to work on Wall Street," Nick explains with that special sureness unique to teenagers. "I want to work for Cantor. I could see myself working there for the rest of my life. I would love to run Cantor Fitzgerald one day."

. . .

Eight-year-old Dylan pressed his nose to the glass, making a circle of fog above the buckets of rocky road and mint chocolate chip. Nick smiled as he watched his little brother deliberate over what flavor to get, as if it were a life-or-death decision. Sydney was happy to be with her brothers but, at twelve, already too mature to get giddy about ice cream. She had always been wise beyond her years, but the last two had aged her even more.

This wasn't just a random evening at the ice cream parlor in Brooklyn Heights. This was a tradition. During Nick's inspiring internship period, he met legendary Cantor CEO Howard Lutnick, whose own brother was killed in the attacks and who had pledged to keep the company going in honor of all those lost. Nick heard that Lutnick had a weekly tradition of taking his two kids, his wife, and his best friend's two kids out for a Thursday evening dinner. He decided that he would start his own tradition with his little brother and sister, who he felt needed a chance to keep their mother's memory alive. Almost weekly, he would take Dylan and Sydney to get ice cream, and they would swap memories, stories, and questions about their mother.

The three siblings, armed with an ice cream cone each, headed down Montague Street and toward the Brooklyn Heights Promenade. The small stretch of walkways, benches, and parks from Remsen Street to Orange Street had an unparalleled view of many of New York City's most famous landmarks: Staten Island, Governors Island, the Statue of Liberty, Ellis Island, South Street Seaport, Fulton Fish Market, the Brooklyn Bridge, and, indeed, Lower Manhattan's forever-altered skyline. As Nick, Dylan, and Sydney settled onto a bench, their gaze stretched across the glittering water of the East River and to the huddle of skyscrapers beyond. The two missing towers loomed like ghosts.

"Nick, is there any chance that our daddy will need to be replaced?" Dylan asked, eyes wide with fear. Dylan was adopted, so he knew that he had, at first, had a biological mom, then his mommy, Catherine, and now a stepmom.

"Daddy's not going anywhere," Nick reassured him. "And your mommy wanted to be your mom for the rest of your life. If there was any way that she could have gotten out, she would have, because she wanted to come home to you."

• • •

Unlike many who lost loved ones on September 11 who preferred to stay away from the media coverage and analysis regarding the attacks, Nick was deeply curious about the events that led to his mother's death. He studied 9/11 documentary specials on television, of which there were dozens within the first few years, looking for clues as to what his mother may have been through in those fateful minutes. "I watch like a detective," he explains. "The saddest part is that I don't get anywhere. I don't know anything more about what might have happened to my mom."

Nick examined the facts over and over again, postulating as to where his mom might have been at exactly 8:46 a.m. eastern standard time—the bathroom? Grabbing a cup of coffee? Sitting at her desk? That was when American Airlines Flight 11 collided with the North Tower, scouring off the thermal insulation on the core columns at temperatures of upward of 1,292 degrees Fahrenheit. But the facts didn't add up to any more comprehensive understanding. Nick still felt at a loss. There was no one left to give an eyewitness account of what it was like on the 105th floor, where his mother had been. "My best guess and my best hope is that it was instant for her," Nick says, definitive and sad.

The alternative—that she suffered, or had some inkling of the magnitude of the violence she was about to face—is too much for him to handle: "You never want to think of your mom being scared. That's the hardest thing for me."

In the early years, Nick dreamed about his mother or the events of September 11 about once a week. His nightmares were filled with terrorist attacks, missed connections with his endangered mom, airplanes, and fire. One night, he was blessed with a wholly different scenario: "I had this one dream where I just hugged my mom for a really, really long time," he remembers. "It was a little scary, because she looked weak, kind of frail, which I think relates to me not knowing what happened to her. But it felt so nice to grab her, to put my face in her hair and just smell her. For those ten minutes, it was real."

Nick was surprised at how visceral his mourning really was. Though he wasn't able to cry, he felt a physical ache. "I think about my mom and my heart literally hurts. It's a very weird sensation," he explains, putting his right hand on his chest. "Right here, my heart hurts."

He also struggled with anxiety—a sense, as he put it, that he had "perpetually forgot something, like something is always missing."

Nick, a self-described "technical kid," initially thought that his acute sadness would last about a year or two. When the second anniversary came and went, he realized that mourning has a far more messy and unpredictable texture than he had once guessed. "I put a time frame on my healing. It's been a big wake-up call, this whole process. You can't work to heal faster. You should let it happen. You shouldn't be forcing anything. Let your body do what it has to do, bit by bit."

Most of us have an inaccurate idea about the grief process. Perhaps no one is as tied to the word "grief" in the public consciousness as Dr. Elisabeth Kübler-Ross, a Swiss-born psychiatrist known for creating the field of thanatology, or near-death studies. After moving to Chicago with her husband in the midsixties, Kübler-Ross was shocked to find that Americans were so conflicted about death as to appear indifferent when she observed them in the hospital setting where she was working. Determined to blow open the conversation about death and dying, Kübler-Ross started interviewing patients who faced an imminent death about the different emotions they were experiencing.

What emerged was the Kübler-Ross model, five distinct and sequential stages of grief: denial, anger, bargaining, depression, and acceptance. The model traveled far and wide via her 1969 book, *On Death and Dying,* which transformed the way we understood grief. For decades to come, Kübler-Ross's model was the accepted wisdom, influencing psychologists, doctors, clergy, and the public at large.

It turns out that as well intentioned as Kübler-Ross was, she was also off the mark. More recent, scientifically rigorous research has proven that grief is less a sequential path through distinct stages and more a process of oscillation—up and down, up and down. In other words, we don't move from one stage on to the next, never to return to that way of relating to our loved one's death. Instead we experience a constant combination of emotions, sometimes feeling lighter and liberated from our grief, and sometimes heavier and more mired in our sadness. The light times make the heavy times bearable.

The pioneer of this new model for understanding grief, Dr. George Bonanno, based his findings on longitudinal studies of people who had lost loved ones—probing their emotional and behavioral reactions over a substantial period of time. What he found was heartening as well as surprising. Our grief doesn't metabolize as we "work" through the stages, like alcoholics recovering from an addiction; our grief dissipates over a period of time as we ride the necessary waves—as Nick so aptly put it, "bit by bit."

A child who loses his or her mother, of course, is in a unique grieving situation. Three thousand kids lost at least one parent in the attacks on September 11. Their average age was nine years old. Tuesday's Children and other organizations were created to help these thousands of young mourners deal with their loss and find camaraderie in one another, but Nick was a bit older than most of the kids who participated in groups like these and was fiercely independent, besides. Instead, he found solace in a group of tight-knit friends, in his new Cantor family, and in his late-night writing sessions, where he resurrected his mom on paper to keep him company in his newly quiet house.

...

Nick finished high school in 2004 with a stellar academic record and a reputation as one of the best squash players in the country, earning him admission into Yale University, his first choice. He promised Sydney and Dylan that, though he couldn't continue to take them out for ice cream every week, they could expect regular phone calls from their big brother.

His third day at Yale happened to coincide with what would have been his mother's forty-ninth birthday. Nick felt a terrible sense of déjà vu. Here he was, at a new school, among people who didn't know him, experiencing a deep, inexplicable sadness unfit for the casual conversations typical of getting-to-know-you banter.

Deciding when and how to tell people about his very personal connection to the events of September 11 was consistently difficult for Nick. He didn't want to be known as "that kid who lost his mom on September 11," yet he didn't overlook the importance of cluing new friends into a huge part of who he was. "It's one of the hardest parts of meeting new people," he says. "It feels like this secret."

Nick hesitated telling people, in large part because he was tired of dealing with the awkwardness of the interaction. "I almost feel embarrassed for them," he explains. "Not that I would do any better, but I don't want to hear any more 'I'm sorrys.'"

This ongoing struggle was put into stark relief when Nick decided to take a small seminar at Yale called Narratives of 9/11, in which students read and discussed novels, articles, and obituaries and watched films related to the terrorist attacks of September 11, 2001. Though the professor knew that Nick had lost his mother in the attacks, none of the other students did. Nick wanted it that way. "It was so valuable to be able to talk to a group of twenty other kids, who are basically my age and don't know my situation," he explains. "I learned so much that I never would have been able to learn if people knew. Some of the things that were said would not have been said."

One day, for example, the students discussed a few selections from the *New York Times*' powerful Portraits of Grief series, in which the *Times* published roughly two hundred words—impressionistic, rather than comprehensive—on every human being who perished in the World Trade Center attacks.

Reading an obituary of one of the Cantor workers, a student expressed that he was sick of hearing about another rich broker. Nick realized that someone could have the same thought reading his mother's obituary. (Her portrait, incidentally, focused on Nick's encounter with the bird while giving his mother's eulogy.) He held his tongue and was strangely grateful to be exposed to this kind of thinking: "Some comments really made me angry: 'These rich traders only care about money. They're a symbol of this capitalist structure. They had it coming.' It was still refreshing to be able to talk about September 11th without people being careful about it."

It was as if, through his anonymity in the Narratives of 9/11 class, Nick was able to experience what it would have been like to relate to the event as just another American—someone with an important connection by nationality, but not a crushing connection by blood.

This was not the only English class that Nick took. Though he majored in economics and spent his summers interning at finance firms, he still felt deeply drawn to writing. "The more I want to get into the financial industry," Nick explains, "the more I want to take classes that have nothing to do with it. I really like to write. I wouldn't mind working on Wall Street for however long and then starting a writing career."

As the years wore on, Nick was increasingly torn about the direction in which his future was moving. On the one hand, he experienced his summer internships in the financial sector as times of powerful reconnection with his mom. In the summer of 2005, he was back at Cantor, this time on the trading desk (a step up from previous years). The head of the trading desk had worked with Nick's mom for ten years, and others on the floor knew her well. They would stop by and check in with Nick, sometimes telling him stories about her no-holds-barred approach to her work. "I knew my mom was successful, but it was so nice to hear little stories," he explains.

The stories, however, paled in comparison to what it would have been like to have his mother around. "It sucks. I'd love to sit down with her and talk about sales, the trades she's done, tricks of the trade . . . it sucks," Nick explains, adding one more time, "It sucks."

As much as he felt drawn to the financial sector—to be close to his mom and to continue her legacy, Nick was slowly realizing that his favorite classes weren't in the economics department, and his moments of feeling most alive involved not numbers, but words. A poetry class during his sophomore year got him writing and remembering his mom in a different way. In the summer that followed, he wrote every single day, getting most of his ideas from his personal journal.

Nick began wrestling with these two sides of himself. Should he go into the fast-paced, high-earning world of finance that his mother had inhabited from nine to five each day, or the more intimate world of words? As graduation approached, he admitted, "I don't really know what I want to do, so that's kind of terrifying."

While he'd done everything necessary over the past eight years to line up a job in finance—the competitive, grueling internships, the networking and academic performance, the anxiety-producing series of interviews, the Series 7 and 63 tests—he just wasn't sure if the path he'd always seen for himself was really the one he should go down. "There's no one there to say, 'Take the road slightly less traveled. Take a chance for a couple of years.'"

For Nick, the decision of what to do with his future was a question not just of what kind of work he might find most fulfilling, but ultimately of what kind of work would honor his mother most powerfully. Going into finance felt like a very direct way to keep her legacy alive: "I think I would feel extremely proud to do something that my mother never got the opportunity to do, in her name, for her. Maybe get to the top. Maybe that's silly. I don't know. I don't know if that's what my mother would have wanted at all, but for whatever reason I feel like I need to do that, to pick up where she left off. She had another eighteen years in her before she retired. I almost feel like I need to put that time in for her."

• • •

In 2008, Nick decided to take a job at Lehman Brothers. Every morning as he took the subway to work, a steaming cup of coffee in one hand, he would imagine that his mom could be sitting across from him, slogging through her daily commute just like him, trying to wake up, just like him. Imagining the ways in which she'd done just these things, felt just these ways, thought about just these things, felt strangely intimate—like they could still share live, not just remembered, moments.

But as much as his first days in the "real world" of work were exciting, as much as he still felt close to his mother, he wasn't happy. The days were long and exhausting. They took a lot out of him. He began to come to terms with the fact that he had been depressed: "I dealt with the immediate aftermath of my mother's death pretty well, and then there were a couple of years when I felt like I should be over it," he explains. "If I could get through my mother's death, I thought, then nothing could depress me ever again. If I got over it, then I should just be happy. Happy forever."

The reality, of course, was very different from that. "I was actually kind of upset a lot of the time. I was numb," Nick admits. "It's almost like I can't even remember the last two years of my life. It's like one long, blurry day."

Nick was not alone. A study appearing in the April 2007 edition of *Biological Psychiatry* found that the rate for psychiatric disorders more than doubled for children who lost a parent in the World Trade Center terrorist attacks on September 11th. More than half of the bereaved children struggled with anxiety, and about 10 percent were diagnosed with major depression disorder.

This is easily understandable when one considers not only the weight of grief more generally, but the weight of grief on a developing child or adolescent. Helen Fitzgerald, author of *The Grieving Teen,* explains: "Fearing the vulnerability that comes with expression, they look for distractions rather than stay with the grief process long enough to find real relief." Staying with that process requires a resiliency that teenagers like Nick, left depleted and disillusioned by their loss, often don't have.

Though Nick was able to acknowledge that he was depressed, he still wasn't able to express his sadness. Nick still didn't cry. "It's more of a deep, aching sadness. It doesn't make me want to cry tears. It makes my body ache. And then anger comes."

Some of the anger that Nick had been harboring for so long—a typical reaction of a grieving child toward the parent who remains, or in the case of a terrorist attack, the culprits—was dissipating. Now it was showing up in unlikely places. Nick had another dream about his mother. In this one, she suddenly returned from a business trip in Russia, where she'd been since September 11, 2001. Nick was furious with her, yelling, "Why the fuck didn't you call me for five years? Why didn't you say good-bye?"

. . .

Novelist C. S. Lewis wrote, "Sorrow turns out to be not a state, but a process. It needs not a map but a history . . . there is something new to be chronicled every day." Such was the case for Nicholas Chirls.

At first, he thought that his midnight poems, the fragments that he wrote about his late mother, the short stories, were mere footnotes to the central narrative that he was living every day: Boy loses his mother, the center of his world, so he enters the center of *her* world and lives out her stolen moments. He was going to pick up where his tough-talking, wheeling-and-dealing mother left off at forty-seven years old. Amid her people, her jargon, her rates and rituals, he would find a continued intimacy. But the story took a sharp turn, as all good ones do. Nick realized that he had written this legacy in too pat a plot.

Nick had always cared about politics and been interested in questions of ethics and justice, but his senior year at Yale had given him some of his first hands-on experiences of trying to do work that really mattered in the world. He'd participated in a program in a disadvantaged neighborhood in New Haven called Squash Haven, in which kids from low-income backgrounds had a chance to play squash, and, in the process, learn discipline and become part of a consistent community of mentors and friends. He longed to feel that sense that his energy was going toward something transformative, not just lucrative.

After a three-week trip to Israel in 2005, he'd also started to think more about how his own experience of having global terrorism shatter his private world was connected to others' experiences. While the families affected by September 11th had been sustained by a tremendous amount of help—financial and emotional—from all over the country, many people are left with nothing to rebuild their lives. Nick explained: "I would love to start an international foundation that would give immediate aid to victims of terrorist attacks all around the world, whether it's in Israel or Lebanon, completely devoid of political bias."

And a trip to China in 2008 had really blown his mind. Nick was awed by watching how this undisputable superpower had grown and changed under such vastly different cultural circumstances from the ones he was used to. Everything he had taken for granted in his American life—from food to fun, body language to national identity—was overturned. Every moment was a learning opportunity, every conversation a cross-cultural exchange. In China, he felt so very far away from the loss and lore of his hometown, as if he'd been transported to a world so far from his own that his past experiences got lost along the way.

Nick's healing process had shifted his world from black-and-white to shades of gray, and then it had expanded exponentially.

While there was no denying the comfort of sitting at his same desk every day, using the same language he had now grown accustomed to, language he knew his mom had once used with ease, being around the same colleagues and friends, there was also something increasingly uncomfortable about it. His profession matched his history, to be sure, but it didn't necessarily align with his passions.

"I would go home at the end of the day and feel as if I wasn't creating. I felt unused," Nick explains. When Lehman Brothers went bankrupt in 2008, Nick saw his exit. He resigned in January of 2009 and began planning an adventure. He felt a strong urge to see new horizons, both literally and within himself. He wanted to get as far from the life he'd known, the identity he'd inherited, as possible.

You can't get much farther than China, which is just where Nick headed and lived from August of 2009 to September of 2010. He played squash with the locals, becoming something of a celebrity. He went to business school to learn about entrepreneurship, a path he was growing more and more interested in taking. He also began writing a memoir about his mother's life and death, and about his relationship with her.

As Nick describes it, "It is the search for my mother, my real mother." Losing a parent at so young an age led Nick to idealize his mother, but even more, to idealize her profession. Though he had once thought that it was his duty, as a son, to live out his mom's legacy in the financial sector, ultimately he realized that his mom would have simply wanted him to be happy. "She would have been the first one to say, 'Cut the crap. Do what you love,'" he realizes.

He's still wrestling with the question of what it is he truly loves, but one thing is clear: The not knowing is a good thing. When that bird landed ever so lightly on his head as he read his mother's eulogy, it shook up everything he knew about life and death, the here-right-now and the hereafter. That confusion marked the beginning of a difficult and important journey for Nick, and as any great philosopher or one great mother, Catherine Ellen Chirls, would tell you, "It's not a matter of what's going to come of it. It's a matter of giving yourself options."

• • •

Nick's mother, though most widely known as a finance expert, also had a deep appreciation for poetry. In fact, every night before Nick went to bed as a boy, his mom would read him a poem by Dinah Mulock Craik, an English novelist and poet from the 1800s:

> *Autumn to winter, winter into spring,*
> *Spring into summer, summer into fall,*
> *So rolls the changing year, and*
> *So we change;*
> *Motion so swift, we know not*
> *That we move.*

One summer, she wrote it on a piece of paper so he could read it before drifting off to sleep and hear her voice in his head when he was away at camp. After his mother died, Nick found the weathered piece of paper and framed it. "It's probably one of my favorite possessions," he explains. "It's in her handwriting, and at the end, it says, 'Sleep tight, Nicholas. I love you. Mommy.'"

Craik's words poignantly capture the journey that Nick—that every mourner, in fact—must take. Rather than plodding through discrete stages of grief, as Kübler-Ross suggested, or stubbornly turning away from any painful memories of the deceased, one faces each day as it comes. Some days are difficult—a dream, like Nick experienced, brings up feelings of abandonment and anger, or something seemingly innocuous sets off a flood of sadness. Some days are easier—one is able to think of one's late friend with a calm smile rather than a piercing stomach pain, a success at school or work feels joyfully connected to the legacy of one's lost love, or perhaps even a whole day goes by when death doesn't pass through the busy activity of a mourning mind.

Before long, these days have piled on top of one another and morphed into weeks, then months, then years, and, as Craik paints it, "So we change." It is often an imperceptible movement, up and down, steadily forward, until we find ourselves living without death as our consistent, erratic companion, but our unforgettable and always available teacher.

The Light at the Top

Brian Lyons

Brian Lyons carries his five-year-old daughter, Patricia, up to bed. He cherishes the small weight of her, her tiny arm draped across his broad shoulder, the way she gives herself fully over to the safety of his arms. After a long day of hauling debris amid a bunch of rough-and-tumble construction workers, the sweet smell of her breath on his neck feels redemptive.

He slowly enters her room—awash in pink—and lays her limp body gently on the bed. He sits beside her for a moment, notices the Irish dancing costumes hanging in the little closet, and situates a stuffed animal close to her body in case she wakes up and feels scared. He takes a deep breath, and as he has since September 11, 2001, he feels the presence of his late brother, Michael.

• • •

Brian was at his latest site assignment on Madison and Twenty-third Street, moving things along as always, when someone on the crew got a page that some planes had flown into the World Trade Center. As a salt-of-the-earth, levelheaded construction manager, Brian wasn't the type to panic. He was usually dressed in a pair of sturdy work boots, jeans, and a T-shirt—he looked like the kind of man who could build a house with his own two hands and some scrap wood, as long as an ice cold Coca-Cola was promised at the end of the day. Life, according to Brian, wasn't about drama. He explains, "As long as you work hard, enjoy simple pleasures, take care of your family, and lend a hand to decent people, you're living right."

As such, on that fateful day, he simply turned to the co-worker next to him and said matter-of-factly, "They're going to need help down there."

He tried calling his brother, Michael, a firefighter with Squad 41, on his cell phone. He'd spoken to him earlier that morning. No answer. He tried the firehouse. No answer. As he stood thirty-eight stories up on the parapet of the building among a sea of other workers, watching the black smoke drift up into the crisp autumn day downtown, it occurred to him that Michael might be down there, or at least on his way. His brother was a helper too. It was how they were raised.

After a little bit of watching, Brian was anxious to *do*. His wife,

Lori, called and urged him to get home, come hell or high water. "Swim if you have to!" she directed. He decided to head uptown to his brother's firehouse in the Bronx to see if he was up there, or if, at the very least, some of the other guys were hanging around and knew what the plan was. But after the long trek up, blending in with the sea of people heading north with briefcases in hand, looks of quiet terror on their faces, he found a completely empty firehouse. No one was left.

If all these guys were helping out, Brian figured, why not him? He quickly hatched a plan—he'd keep on walking north until he could hop on a Metro-North train and get to his brother's house in Westchester, where he knew he could find some of Michael's extra gear in the basement. He'd suit up, grab Michael's extra ID (despite being eight years apart, they looked enough alike to pass for each other—both stocky guys with that pale, Irish skin and round, jolly faces), and just head down there. He would see what he could see, and help in whatever way he could help.

After a stop at his own home where he kissed Lori good-bye and fended off her protests, Brian headed out. He drove down the eerily empty FDR Drive and headed west to the World Trade Center site. A parkway that normally carries upward of 175,000 cars through Lower Manhattan, and all the noise and pollution that they produce, was suddenly a nearly silent passageway for one determined man.

Brian hardly had the energy to notice how bizarre it all was— driving alone on the FDR, a road that he had cursed more than once on other bumper-to-bumper occasions. His entire body was engaged in his mission—his heart was beating fast, his eyes were watching the smoky air drift by, his digestion had slowed down to a quiet grumble. He knew that New York was falling apart all around him, but all he could see was the narrow path he'd carved out in his mind that led straight to his brother.

Thanks to his brother's ID, he got through all the checkpoints that Tuesday morning, parked his car on the corner of Pine and Church Streets, and headed—counter to the stream of people searching for safety—toward the site. "It was like a war zone," he remembers. Fires were still burning. Paper and dead bodies covered the ground. Piles of steel were everywhere. Brian took a deep breath, surveying the carnage in every direction. He decided to walk the entire perimeter of the demolished site, so as to get a better sense of the scale of the damage and need.

It quickly became very obvious that it would be difficult to find his brother amid all the chaos. There were police and firefighters everywhere, everyone trying to coordinate getting to the injured and buried people still trapped in the ruins. Massive machines were already moving piles of steel to help rescue workers get in to find survivors. In the meantime, he decided, he would just help out. As he walked, he gave himself a little pep talk: "Just one grain of sand. That's all I've got to do. If I can do something to the best of my ability, add one grain of sand to the bucket, then I can help the common goal."

He wouldn't leave the site for three full weeks.

· · ·

Brian's firefighter brother Michael was the youngest of four sons and, as a result, had the most eyes and expectations on him as he was coming of age in the Lyons family. "We all wanted to make him what we weren't," Brian explained. "We wanted to make sure he got good schooling, went to a good college, and he was good in sports."

Stickball was king on the streets of Yonkers in the sixties and seventies when the boys were growing up. "There would be ten, twenty, thirty kids on the corner at one time," Brian remembers. "You had generations—my older brother and friends, me and my friends . . ." They would spend hours playing games and talking trash.

The Lyons family immigrated to the United States in 1957, after a decade of economic depression and political violence in their home country of Ireland. Brian was born in 1960. Michael, dubbed "the moon baby," was born on July 20, 1969—one day before Neil Armstrong first stuck an American flag in that silvery orb far, far away.

All the boys were raised in the Catholic Church and taught to be pious, helpful, and scrappy—always looking for opportunities to make a buck. From a very young age, Brian would wander onto local construction sites and ask if he could lend a hand, "hoping for a dollar to get something to eat." It was during these long, hot days of summer that he first learned about construction work. On rare trips to Lower Manhattan as a teenager, he remembers marveling at the World Trade towers, which he viewed as feats of construction, symbols of patriotism and power. Brian explains, "I admired the Twin

Towers since I was a little kid. Just like you want your baseball team to win the World Series, you want your city to have the biggest, best building in the world. That's how I thought about those towers."

Brian wasn't very drawn to school, so he figured that he'd join the service instead, even if his heart wasn't really in that either. "I was just a kid going to boot camp," he remembers. "They do everything bad to you." But there was a silver lining to all that harsh treatment: "I got stationed in Alaska for a year and half. I was sailing around the North Pacific at nineteen years old. It was really good."

As Brian was wandering around the world as part of the service, Michael went on to Manhattan College, where he studied mechanical engineering. "He's got a good head on his shoulders," Brian explains.

Brian finally settled back into the area in the late eighties, at which time he met Lori—a bright young business school student at the time. He proposed to her at the World Trade Center restaurant, Windows on the World, on September 12, 1989, and they were married in 1990. They were excited to start a family right away but weren't able to conceive their first child, Elizabeth, until 1995, followed by Patricia in 1998—right around the same time that Michael started his own family with his new wife, Elaine. Their first daughter, Caitlin, was born in 2000.

This was also the time that Michael became a firefighter. There were very few engineering jobs when Michael graduated, but his name came up on the list for the FDNY—he'd taken the test his senior year in high school—so he jumped at the chance.

Michael and Brian were very close, coming up with all sorts of entrepreneurial schemes, even a baby-bottle business. When Michael decided he wanted to renovate his house, Brian teamed up with him. On their many drives to Home Depot and in almost daily phone calls, they cemented the plans for the renovation and carried it out, side by side. They mourned the loss of their parents together. Their daughters were destined to be playmates. Their wives were friends. Everything seemed to have turned out as the Irish blessing foretold that it would:

MAY YOU ALWAYS HAVE WALLS FOR THE WINDS, A ROOF FOR THE RAIN, TEA BESIDE THE FIRE, LAUGH-TER TO CHEER YOU, THOSE YOU LOVE NEAR YOU, AND ALL YOUR HEART MIGHT DESIRE. MAY ST. PATRICK GUIDE YOU WHEREVER YOU GO, AND GUIDE YOU IN WHATEVER YOU DO—AND MAY HIS LOVING PROTEC-TION BE A BLESSING TO YOU ALWAYS. MAY THE ROAD RISE TO MEET YOU, MAY THE WIND BE ALWAYS AT YOUR BACK. MAY THE SUN SHINE WARM UPON YOUR FACE, THE RAINS FALL SOFT UPON YOUR FIELDS AND, UNTIL WE MEET AGAIN, MAY GOD HOLD YOU IN THE PALM OF HIS HAND.

• • •

Brian slept in his car, ate donated sandwiches, drank copious amounts of donated coffee, and worked for three straight weeks following September 11, 2001. Whatever project he found that needed doing—no matter how seemingly mundane—he would attach him-self to it and make sure he saw it through from start to finish. Whether it was removing a small section of debris, in hopes that there was an air pocket below, or making a path to a particular sec-tion of the site where rescue workers were concentrating, he was there to see the project through. He knew no one working alongside him but quickly made friends with other bighearted people trying to move the rescue effort along. Brian's steady demeanor was a huge asset in the midst of such traumatic work; rescue workers were attracted to both his calming presence and his capable hand.

Brian would call a few times a day, giving both his wife and Michael's wife updates on what was going on down there. Elaine and Michael's home had become a bustling center where family mem-bers came through, bringing food and prayers for Michael's safety. Sometimes they would take the girls to Chuck E. Cheese's or Carvel to keep them away from the steady stream of sobering conversation among the adults. Their sprawling extended family held out hope that Brian would call any minute with news of Michael's rescue. Lori worried about Brian—she couldn't imagine what kinds of things he was experiencing down there. But she tried to keep her worries, small in comparison with Elaine's, at bay and focus on finding Michael. Later, she admitted to Brian that she was absolutely terri-fied for his safety.

For three weeks the family prayed and gathered, and Brian worked and waited for any sign that his brother might be alive, trapped in the rubble somewhere as if living in a postapocalyptic pocket of air and safety somewhere beneath the surface of rubble. Michael was "the moon baby," after all; maybe he'd figured out some way to survive in quiet darkness.

And then, one bright October morning—as if the people working there were waking up from a collective dream—the mood on-site dramatically shifted. "I remember it was eight o'clock and the sun was out, nice sunny day, and the whole site was at a different pace," Brian remembers. "Everything was one notch down, much slower. Everyone just knew—there really isn't [anyone] alive now. We're still working hard, but it wasn't the same intensity of trying to save someone trapped under a piece of steel."

For Brian, the shift meant a chance to slow down, but it also meant something much more profound. "That was the moment I knew," he explains. "I looked at my watch and it was 8:01. Whatever date it was, I knew we weren't going to find him alive or anyone else alive." The effort went from being a project of rescue to one of recovery. They were no longer looking for survivors; they were looking for remains. Michael was dead.

It was at the end of that day that Brian finally decided it was time to go home and kiss and hug Lori and the girls, and tell Elaine— almost nine months pregnant—that the father of her children, her husband, her childhood sweetheart, wasn't coming home.

• • •

After breaking the news to Elaine, he retreated to the warmth and comfort of his own little family. It was nice to be home, to feel the warm bodies of his little girls and the loving embrace of his wife, but by four thirty the next morning, Brian was back at the Brewster train station, waiting for the five a.m. train. It was a foggy October morning. Everything was very still and peaceful. Only one other man stood on the platform.

He looked to be in his fifties or sixties. They struck up a casual conversation. Then the man said, apropos of nothing, "Don't worry. Everything will come out all right. Things will work out for the best." Brian was stunned. He hadn't told him anything about where he was headed or where he had been.

The man went on, "Things are screwed up, but it should work out." Despite his confusion at how this man could possibly know anything about what he was dealing with, Brian found his words, his presence, strangely consoling.

The train appeared in the distance, moving toward them. Brian said, "Nice talking to you," and reached out his hand. "I'm Brian."

"Nice talking to you too," the man responded, taking his hand and shaking it with a warm sureness. "I'm Michael Lyons."

Brian, stunned to the core, got on one train while the man with his dead brother's name got on another.

• • •

The recovery effort was tedious, backbreaking, and traumatic, but Brian felt deeply committed to helping with any- and everything. He was especially focused on finding his brother's remains. "I felt I had a responsibility to bring his remains home," Brian explained.

"Because of my nature, and the nature of the beast that was down there—organized chaos, if you will—I really felt that they needed someone of my stature to organize some of these things. I couldn't sleep at night knowing someone down there might screw it up." Brian had ample experience managing complex construction projects and prided himself on his capacity to keep things moving on schedule, with integrity and a sense of team unity.

He put off his sadness surrounding his loss by toiling day in and day out, eighteen-hour days, no time for tears or memories. He told himself that Michael would want him down there, helping out, making sure things were done properly. He reassured Lori that his absence was only temporary, that he would have a regular schedule again once he found whatever remains existed of Michael and his buddies from Squad 41.

What allowed Brian to sustain such long, arduous hours? Psychologists have been investigating the nature of human resilience since the late seventies. Up until that time, many researchers felt that the only respectable or serious focus of study was on pathology—essentially, what went wrong with people's psyches. Countless research dollars and ounces of typewriter ink went into investigating dysfunction. But just as a political and social change shifted the tectonic plates of American life in the tumultuous seventies, the field of psychology also changed at that time—the psychological version of "make love, not war"; study what is restorative in the human psyche, not just what is potentially destructive. Resiliency theory was born.

In 1979, psychologist S. C. Kobasa argued that resilience was related to three healing beliefs: (1) control—that one can influence circumstances (in contrast to adopting a victimized identity); (2) commitment—that one expects to find purpose and passion through one's own resourcefulness; and (3) challenge—that one pursues growth even when it's hard, knowing that this leads to greater fulfillment in the long run. Brian, it seems, is a poster child for this hardy response to trauma and loss.

He was also buoyed by fate. Eerie events, like that which transpired on the train platform in Putnam County, continued to happen, making him feel as if his work at Ground Zero was a matter of destiny. "I don't believe in ESP or UFOs or nothing," Brian explained, "but very, very weird things happened down there."

The Swiss psychologist Carl Jung explains such happenings through his concept of "synchronicity." Jung explains: "Meaningful coincidences are unthinkable as pure chance—the more they multiply and the greater and more exact the correspondence is, the more they can no longer be regarded as pure chance, but, for the lack of causal explanation, have to be thought of as meaningful arrangements."

These inexplicable moments are experienced not only by those in mourning, of course—just ask a starry-eyed couple how they met and you'll likely hear a tale of synchronicity. But for someone trying to process a recent loss, someone aching for a sense of connection to a loved one who has been torn from their daily lives in one brutal swoop, synchronicity ensures a continuation of the relationship.

Whether real or imagined—who can possibly know?—these defining moments are opportunities for comfort and wonder.

On Thanksgiving morning, Brian had yet another ineffable experience. He watched as a machine dug up a huge batch of identification cards and sent them flying through the air. On a whim, he grabbed one, and then a strong thought flashed through his head: "I know I'm going to read this thing, and it's going to say Michael Lyons." Indeed, it was his brother's ID card.

On St. Patrick's Day, at around five p.m., Brian and a couple of guys from Squad 41 who hadn't been on duty that fateful day, two of Michael's dearest friends, were digging in the same general area as where the ID card had shown up months earlier. All of a sudden, a piece of hard metal hit Brian in the foot. He looked down to see a Halligan bar—a tool commonly used by firefighters and law enforcement to pry, twist, or force entry—with Squad 41 etched onto it. "I just knew my brother had been carrying that Halligan that day," Brian said. Michael was often the one to grab the Halligan for his team.

As he held it in his hand, feeling the weight of the cold metal and experiencing a wave of relief, a light snow began to fall. "I realized that there was a force that kept me going from 9/11 until St. Patrick's Day," Brian explains. "The instant it started snowing, it was like a switch went off inside, as if everything was drained from me."

But Brian and Michael's friends didn't give up just yet. They kept digging in that exact spot. Just before midnight, they found a very hot area filled with ashes and bones. Later on the next day, they found a Squad 41 helmet. Within three days, they had recovered every tool, bone fragment, and all the remains they could find in the area. The remains went to the medical examiner's office to be identified. Brian brought the tools back to the firehouse, where the surviving squad members laid everything out. Just about every tool was there, except for the head of a solitary ax. To his great relief and honor, the squad gave Brian the Halligan, saying it was his right to keep it in honor and memory of his brother.

"That was huge closure," Brian explained. He had fulfilled his responsibility of finding what was left of his baby brother, a sacred promise he'd made to himself. (None of Michael's physical remains were ever found.)

At Michael's memorial service, Brian recounted that his brother had always regretted having missed "the action" with the 1993 bombing at the World Trade Center. "Everyone wants to get the big fire," Brian explained. "So when the towers were on fire, I knew Michael was so excited to get there. I could picture him, getting out of the fire engine, grabbing his Halligan, and running into that building. I know he was full steam ahead, trying to get in there and accomplish something he had in his heart."

• • •

Roman lyric poet Horace wrote, "Adversity has the effect of eliciting talents, which in prosperous circumstances would have lain dormant." He could have been speaking of Brian, who in the process of pitching in at Ground Zero found both a mission and a new identity. He had always worked in construction, of course, but the leadership that emerged from within during his time on the recovery effort brought his professional life to a new level. He was asked to stay on as one of the key managers overseeing the PATH Restoration Project from August of 2002 to November of 2003.

Every morning, he would facilitate a coordination meeting at nine a.m. between the fifteen subcontractors and the PATH and MTA teams. They would go over the agenda, talk about various safety issues, cover any labor questions (e.g., Who is working today? How long are they working?), go over all the systems (fire alarms, elevators, plumbing, heating, sewer, drainage, etc.), and discuss how the track work and other reconstruction efforts were coming along. Brian would write down any outstanding issues on the board and assign people to follow up. It was like he was the choreographer of an incredibly intricate dance involving hundreds of laborers, thousands of tons of steel, and the dream of a restored transportation hub downtown.

Brian believed that his brother would have been proud of him, that he would have seen the new job as a great accomplishment. "It's something Michael and I would have talked about," he said. "It's like he guided me right here—the whole way through, the whole process." When they placed the first beam in the temporary PATH train of the "bathtub"—what the workers called the pit of Ground Zero—in August of 2002, Brian wrote, MICHAEL LYONS, SQUAD 41, on it.

The project wasn't easy, as it was on an accelerated schedule. Brian had to face down some stress, deal with lots of conflicts along the way, work long, hard hours. On tough days on the site, he would give Michael a hard time in his head: *I'm walking through the mud and the freezing cold. Jesus Christ, Lyons, look what you got me into. I'm down here because of you, you dope.*

On the final Friday of the project, Brian traded his usual construction outfit for a freshly pressed suit and tie. The crew was shocked to see Brian stroll in dressed in such fancy attire. "Most of 'em had never seen me not in my construction boots," he says, smiling.

In that last morning meeting, he talked about his personal journey of going from a guy just looking for his brother on September 11 to a leader in the rebuilding effort. He reviewed some of the highlights of the project from beginning to end. He talked about his favorite quotation from football coach Vince Lombardi: "I firmly believe that any man's finest hour, the greatest fulfillment of all that he holds dear, is that moment when he has worked his heart out in a good cause and lies exhausted on the field of battle—victorious." The workers had seen to it that Ground Zero—their "battlefield"— was no longer just a site of carnage, but one of new construction and new life.

• • •

Ironically, the very day that they flipped the lights on in the PATH station, Brian began to feel the darkness of his own soul. A dread, an emptiness, an anxiety, began to creep in. Slowing down meant facing himself and the emotions that had been building up over the course of three years of all-consuming toil.

"You can't get emotional when you have jobs to do," Brian explains. "The first couple of years, I felt like I had a job to do. We were doing recovery and then the initial rebuilding. To get emotional and show emotion would take away from the job at hand. Now I'm not there, it's pretty quiet. Now some of this emotion is coming up." Brian, in a sense, delayed his grief by doing such tireless, all-consuming work. It didn't begin to hit him until the spring of 2004.

Brian bravely got help from one of the agencies supporting Project Liberty, the leading organization in mental health services for those affected by 9/11 and the largest crisis-counseling program ever launched in the United States. Project Liberty hired close to five thousand New Yorkers and trained them to provide crisis intervention in all of the counties affected by the attacks. Running for three years, the program leveraged a total of $152 million from federal agencies and wound up seeing 1.2 million people. Dr. April Naturale, the trauma specialist who directed Project Liberty, explains, "The goals were to [teach patients to] develop resilience, to help people integrate what they'd learned into their lives, to strengthen communities and decrease isolation. We wanted to build hope."

So many people, particularly rescue workers, suffered the aftermath of September 11th years later. Naturale attests that it often takes someone a year to even begin to heal from a major loss.

Brian described his feelings in 2004: "I can usually do eight things at once, but I don't have enough 'umph' right now. Maybe it's the depression coming on." Indeed, he received a diagnosis of post-traumatic stress disorder (PTSD) and began attending weekly therapy appointments to discuss his flashbacks of the carnage that he had witnessed during the recovery efforts and his ongoing symptoms of disassociation, depression, anger, and hypervigilance—startling, for example, at the site of a shoe on the floor because it triggers memories of severed feet lying around at Ground Zero in the immediate aftermath. The New York State Department of Health, which studied data from the World Trade Center Health Registry, found that one in eight first responders suffered from PTSD as a result of work done at Ground Zero.

Brian's PTSD manifested itself in a variety of ways. He would lose focus during conversations and sometimes not even remember what he'd said a few hours later. He and Lori fought far more than usual because Brian's temper had gotten much worse. He sometimes tucked the girls in at night, hoping they would think everything was normal, and then head out to his truck in the driveway to sleep, intent on avoiding any more emotional uproars with his wife for the rest of the night. One day, shortly before Christmas, he fired his entire team at work because he felt they weren't cooperating with his requests. He just lost it and let them all go. For cheerful, easygoing Brian, these changes were intolerable.

Therapy was a new experience for him, but he faced it bravely nonetheless. "For me, its time to look inward, make sure that I'm fine," Brian explained in 2004. "I have to make sure I don't have any lasting problems, and if I do, I can deal with them appropriately."

Elaine, Michael's widow, also struggled to heal. Brian explained, "Elaine is still hurting. They were childhood sweethearts. That's very,

very hard to get over. She still has the everyday task of raising the children." Brian and his family visit Elaine and her children often. The cousins, all close in age, are good friends. Their ebullient energy helps keep the mood light, even when the adults reminisce about Michael.

Elaine too felt like she saw signs of Michael in various strange coincidences that popped up—she would look at the clock right at 9:11, or she would think about Michael and a picture of him would fall from a shelf in the closet, seemingly on its own. Brian, hoping to affirm some of what Elaine was experiencing, told her about his strange sense that Michael was with him every time he tucked his girls into bed. "After I told her," Brian explains, "I never felt that way again." It was as if saying it out loud had stripped the experience of its mystical meaning.

. . .

In the years that followed, Brian went through a lot. He suffered from a life-threatening case of diverticulitis that put him in the hospital three times, each time pushing him to contemplate his own mortality. He continued to struggle with the fallout of PTSD. He worried that he might never feel energized or happy-go-lucky again. Brian's next construction project, away from the Ground Zero family, felt foreign and meaningless in comparison. He reflected, "It was a whole big change right there, leaving a job I was at for three years, moving to a new company. I didn't know anybody there, had to learn new faces, make new friends. That's a big change to swallow. It was tough to get acclimated with everyone."

But time did heal. By the end of 2005, after a year of therapy and plenty of downtime, Brian felt that his mental health was markedly improved. "I'm much better," he explains. "Now my relationship with my wife is very, very good. We've become stronger as a unit. I'm more sensitive to my wife's needs. We talk a lot about different issues. Our relationship has become more fulfilling." One of the subtle successes of Project Liberty was introducing otherwise therapy-averse "tough guys"—like Brian and so many other rescue workers—to a new emotional vocabulary and the capacity to label and work with their own thoughts, feelings, and behaviors.

Dealing with his PTSD also meant refocusing on some of his most dearly held values, foremost among them quality time with his family. When Brian's eldest daughter made her Communion in May of 2003, and his youngest in 2007, he was deeply touched: "It was obviously a big thing," he says, the trademark look of a proud father painted across his face.

Brian also found great strength and solace in his annual camping trips with his wife and daughters. For ten days they would head out into the wilderness and spend quality time side by side. "There's no phone, no TV, no electricity," Brian describes. "We just sit by the beach, sit by the campfire. I go fishing. My family is more important than anything."

Eventually, Brian was able to get an assignment back down at Ground Zero, supervising all of the electrical work for the Freedom Tower. Then he became the general superintendent of construction for Towers 3 and 4. The shift, which was a promotion of sorts, helped his emotional mental state considerably. He felt that after all the destruction of the past few years, he was really part of rebuilding something for the future. It also made him feel closer to his brother again: "Every day I'm working on the site, I look down at where I found Michael's remains." Two or three times a week, Brian made an effort to actually stand in the area where he found the Halligan bar and say a prayer for his lost brother.

Being down at the site also helped Brian reconnect with what he perceived to be his new calling in life: contributing to the rebuilding of Ground Zero so that generations to come would see his brother and others memorialized and have a new symbol of patriotism—the Freedom Tower, just like the towers he had grown up with. "Patricia, my eight-year-old, is in third grade," he explains, "and she says she can't wait to go to school and tell everyone, 'My dad is building the biggest building in the world.'"

Brian realizes that he began working at Ground Zero when he was forty-one years old and probably won't finish with the Freedom Tower until he is at least fifty-five. It has literally become "a life's work." When it's finished, Brian explains, "I'm staying there until we can put that last lightbulb on top."

. . .

As Brian's youngest daughter, Patricia, got older, her bedtime ritual changed. Instead of slinging her over his shoulder, Brian sits beside her as she struggles to make out the words on a page of one of her books. A new reader, she delights in sounding out a word she's never encountered before. Brian explains with absolute reverence: "She reads for twenty minutes. I sit by the side of the bed. Last night I was thinking, 'This is more important than building Ground Zero or making a good salary. You could have no money and be homeless, but your daughter is reading to you, struggling on one or two words that she needs your help on. You talk about the story. You finish two chapters and then it's time for bed.' *That's* important to me."

Though this bedtime ritual no longer evokes the presence of his brother, he revels in it nonetheless. Even in the shadow of those two ghostly towers, even in comparison with the innumerable hours and backbreaking labor that Brian has put into what is truly a sacred site for him, nothing compares with the sweet smell and warm feeling of having his daughter's arms and legs draped over him as the darkness sets in, listening to her little voice stumble mightily over new words.

Losing Michael, his dearest friend and little brother, was—most of all—a clarifying experience for Brian. As is the case for so many others who are forced to mourn too soon someone who matters so much, Brian became acutely aware of what is most important in life.

As we ride the roller coaster of mourning, we are compelled to steady ourselves by focusing in on what actually constitutes a well-lived life. We know that we cannot prevent loss, having experienced it firsthand, but this only illuminates our incentive to make the most of the time we have with those who are most dear to us. We will mourn someday. There's no preventing it. But today, we, like Brian, can choose to treasure the little moments that may seem insignificant but are in fact the marrow of a good life.

Never Forget to Do Your Part

Charles Cook

As Helen Cook Price rode a train down south from New York City to her native Baltimore, her thoughts were with her husband in Italy, who was doing his part for his country. He was fighting for America in World War II. Helen was an attractive and independent woman of Welsh and Native American ancestry with long dark hair she wore in braids.

Her grandson, Charles, sat beside her, a mere boy but taking it all in with his kind brown eyes. He was playing with the curtains, trying to get a glimpse out the window at the speeding landscape. "You can't move the curtains!" Helen told the boy. "The curtains have to stay drawn." Blackout rules during the war also applied to trains.

After finishing her last cigarette, Helen picked up the empty pack and began smoothing out the foil from the inside of the box. "What are you doing, Tana?" Charles asked, ever the curious child and also mindful not to call Helen "Grandma" (she claimed that she was too young to be one so shouldn't have to suffer the name).

"Even though we're not on the front lines, boy, we're at war. We got to save these foils for the war effort. Never forget to do your part."

It was a lesson he would never forget.

. . .

The morning of September 11, Charles Cook, now sixty years old, woke up at home in his Harlem apartment. The man known as "C.C." to his many friends and acquaintances was born and raised in that very same neighborhood. His childhood there was filled with a sense of real community. During the forties and fifties, doors were open to friends up and down the block: "All my friends and I, we intertwined," he wistfully recalls. "We just went from house to house without worrying about knocking on each other's doors. We just walked in each other's houses because we were all a close-knit family."

Things had dramatically changed over the years. The neighborhood had suffered decades of blight and devastation brought on by drugs and gang violence. But friendship, community, and good fun were still landmarks of his life uptown.

On a normal day Charles could look forward to meeting up with friends at the park to challenge them to the highly strategic card game known as pinochle. He loved to challenge them to a higher-stakes version of the game, "double-deck, cutthroat pinochle," sometimes into the night and all through the weekend. His early retirement from driving trains for the Metropolitan Transit Authority (due to a herniated disc) meant that anytime was a good time to start another tournament.

He could still remember Tana with a beer in her hand, cursing like a sailor and whipping him at pinochle. As an adult, when Charles would drive Tana back down to visit her cousins in Baltimore, they would team up to whip their southern relatives.

On that fateful morning, however, Charles's life would make a turn far, far from the leisurely pace of the past couple of years. He turned on the television to a local channel soon after waking up. He recalls watching an interview with a "probie," a rookie firefighter, on his first day out in the Wall Street area. The camera panned to a shot of the World Trade Center. A moment later, a low-flying plane soared across the screen and crashed suddenly into one of the towers. Charles sat, stunned for a moment, his mouth agape, and immediately thought, *That's no accident.*

Charles also remembers the static distress calls that could then be heard on television from the firefighters' scanners. "Alert! Alert!" was the summons, and then came the Pavlovian screams of a group of people trained to act without question: "We're coming! We're coming!" yelled the cavalry over the airwaves.

Charles wanted as much information as he could gather, so he turned the radio on as well. A man was actually calling from inside one of the burning buildings, describing the unbearable heat. He was trying to find an exit but kept getting pushed back by flames. The man dropped the phone, but the radio host stayed on the line.

In a few breathless moments, the man came back and said he'd found a woman amid the smoke. The man's tone was much calmer now. He claimed that they were both fine and that they loved their families. Then silence. Not a second later, newscasters on the television reported that a man and a woman had jumped from a window, holding hands.

We're at war, Charles thought.

. . .

"The only time I traveled out of the country was courtesy of the United States Army, 1959 'til about '62," Charles states proudly. Charles was part of the 299th Combat Engineer Battalion. His military occupational specialties were water purification and demolition. During the heightened years of the cold war, he and his fellow soldiers were stationed near Frankfurt as defensive support for West Germany from the communist East.

As part of their training missions, the military engineers perfected several types of bridging techniques, including building floating bridges out of inflatable rubber rafts known as pontoons. Charles is proud of having helped his company break the record for fastest bridging across the Rhine River.

Charles's military service ended without his having seen actual combat. Not that he had wanted to. His grandfather, Tana's husband, had not made it back from war. He was buried in Italy, where he had fallen.

Once home, back in Harlem, Charles went through his belongings. He noticed that some of his clothes had been given away. Most of all he missed the blue and orange sweater Tana had knit for him as a present when he turned fifteen. He didn't bother her about it, though. He already knew nothing lasted forever, with the exception of her generosity, which just went on and on. In fact, Tana let him move in with her then. There was nowhere else Charles felt more welcome.

. . .

When the first tower collapsed, Charles stopped watching and started acting. He worried about his daughter, Vicky, an epidemiologist working downtown with the city's department of health. He knew his two younger sons, Charles Jr. and Dwayne, were not near the towers, nor was their mother, Carol, from whom Charles had been separated for many years, but with whom he maintained a good relationship.

His thoughts came back to the firefighters who had been rushing to the scene only to meet their deaths. The people would need help, and help had just died. He thought, in horror, of the victims, his fellow New Yorkers, and suddenly the island of Manhattan shrank in his mind. Harlem was not far north anymore, and all he needed to get to Wall Street was a pair of comfortable shoes. He put on an old pair of pants and rushed down the stairs. There was work to do "down there."

He made his way down the steps of his building on 147th Street with the sturdiness of someone decades younger. As Charles walked downtown through the familiar neighborhood, there was no time to notice the newly planted trees lining the streets in front of regal-looking brownstones. Despite his average build and graying afro, his quickened steps and determined gaze gave a sense of toughness built up from the inside, like the concentric rings inside a tree.

All public transportation was at a standstill, so the subway was not an option. Charles proceeded to make his way down by foot from 147th Street. Just south of Harlem, his journey took him through Central Park, where he saw people scampering in every direction except south. Then a police officer approached him. "Everybody's coming uptown!" exclaimed the officer.

"Yes, I know," Charles replied. "I'm going downtown."

"What are you going to do?"

"I'm going to work."

"You are going to work?" the officer asked in disbelief.

To which Charles stated, "Yeah, I'm going to the World Trade Center."

Before reaching the site, Charles made sure to stop at the bank to get some cash, never one to be caught unprepared. He foresaw needing to buy boots to get through the rubble, but he would have to get them later. He had to get down there as quickly as possible.

The scene where the Twin Towers once stood was chaotic and surreal. He saw haze, papers, an entire universe dismantled. He saw ash, the lost, the broken. Charles knew how odd it was to be reminded of Coney Island, but the street was nothing but gray sand, an ersatz beach. He took in the terror of the men and women running from the rubble. Their tears made tracks on their dust-covered faces.

Charles had arrived in the afternoon, just as firefighters were being evacuated from 7 World Trade Center, another building that had caught fire upon the North Tower's collapse. About twenty minutes after five p.m., Charles was a live witness to this third building's collapse.

The giant cloud of smoke lingered up above the site, its reach stretching gradually along the city and beyond the Hudson River. Charles watched a group of rescue workers at street level do the unimaginable—find life among the death and destruction. The hope of finding any more survivors waned as Charles saw body bag after body bag zipped up.

His attention was then drawn to "the hole," where pockets formed amid the rubble would hopefully yield stranded victims holding on to life. Charles knew he'd have no use for his claustrophobia. The energy of the numerous volunteers already there gave him the confidence to do his part: *If these guys can do it, I can do it!* And that was how it began for Charles: He picked up a pail of water and made his way into the lion's mouth, down into "the hole."

• • •

Says Vicky of her father, Charles, "9/11 totally transformed him. Prior to that, he had aged physically but was still very much a young man." Now, with newfound purpose and maturity, she says his focus is on giving to others.

At first, Charles had even hesitated to let his family know that he was volunteering at Ground Zero. "I wasn't gonna tell no one," he says. "I didn't want nobody worrying about me." But days into his service in September of 2001, Charles ran into Vicky on the subway. She had been in Queens, comforting a friend who lost her husband in the attacks. Charles had made his way to midtown to clear his mind and his lungs and to buy some disposable cameras for fellow volunteers.

While on the platform, Charles was writing his name on the tag of his jacket when he heard a familiar woman's voice say, "Why are you writing your name on your jacket?"

Once he recognized her, he explained what he had been doing and that there was nothing that would keep him from heading back to that hole.

"But why do you have to go back down there?" she asked.

"You just can't leave," was the only answer Charles could muster. He felt as if every volunteer at Ground Zero had become his brother and sister. Vicky went on to her job with the New York State Department of Health, but not before Charles urged her to use a respirator. She remembers asking him, "But what about you?" He just shrugged his shoulders and boarded the train.

• • •

Charles walked uptown, cash in pocket, to buy a pair of much-needed boots after it became clear—in his first twenty-four hours on-site—that he would need them amid all the rubble. Just moments after diving back into work, new boots gleaming in the autumn sun, a beam fell on Charles's foot and fractured his big toe. The pain shot through his spine. Blinding pain. He was offered medical treatment by a worried volunteer. "For a toe?" he asked, eyes wide. "Nah. Ain't nothing. Pain is good. It means that I'm alive." Truth be told, the pain was too much. His swollen toe had turned black and Charles soon needed medical attention.

Back at Ground Zero after a quick visit to the hospital, Charles took a break from tough manual labor and joined a team that was dispensing clothing. He slept on the street that night with other volunteers in front of the Brooks Brothers store at One Liberty Plaza. The store's welcome mat was their only padding. The next day they were offered a change of clothes inside the store. The fancy-suited mannequins were cleared from the destruction. The building was about to be turned into a morgue.

They could hear the movement of cranes above lifting the over-laid ruins of the fallen towers with utmost caution. Dislodging any piece could cause the rest of the pile to crumble, a risk the volunteers were well aware of. Charles could feel the rubble shifting once in a while, releasing more and more dust.

That was a moment that Charles would never forget in those early days right after the attacks, when he first felt the dust filling his lungs. He turned to a fellow responder beside him and said, "We fucked!" That was a fact, and they all knew it. Charles coughed and could not clear his throat—just the beginning of the sticky feeling in his chest, like glass cutting through him with every breath.

The first responders didn't need doctors or researchers to tell them what they already knew: The dust would make them sick. And yet they could not walk away.

. . .

"They slapped us in the face!" Charles often states emphatically when asked to explain his actions on September 11. Dr. Helen Fisher, an anthropologist with a keen eye for examining the research on the biological basis for personality traits, seems to be describing Charles when she writes, "Individuals with high levels of testosterone are more likely than other types to dash into a burning building to save a stranger, attack an armed bully with nothing but their fists, or brave a hurricane or tornado to save an abandoned dog. And when asked what prompted them to perform their act of courage, these heroes often say they were barely thinking."

Charles, however, finds that his courage that day was in part due to his strict upbringing in the hands of a father who "did not spare the rod." His father made him take a bold, fighting stance in the face of an attack and keep a stiff upper lip.

As a schoolboy in Harlem's St. Aloysius Catholic School, Charles would often get into fights. "Well, my father encouraged it," he explains with some reticence. "He said, 'I wanna make sure when you get older, you don't fear nobody,' and I fear no man." His father also used to box, and he taught the young Charles, who then went on to box in amateur leagues during his army years.

His father's unconventional parenting style, however, sometimes went to extremes, like when Charles was sent to school wearing shorts during the freezing cold of winter. He was old and tall enough for knickers, and it wasn't that his family couldn't afford them, but he was expected to forgo momentary comfort in pursuit of larger goals, in this case his father's regimen of making strong men out of his two boys.

His younger brother sought shelter in his mother's arms. Charles's mother was from Jamaica and a long line of fierce, rebellious women. Charles realized he was not her favorite and so turned to Tana when he needed comfort or advice. Tana, after all, commanded the most respect from him. Charles had seen her slap her own son, his father, who used to whip *him*. It was clear who was at the top of the Cook hierarchy. That, and the fact that Tana always bought good, comfortable shoes for the flat-footed Charles made her the absolute best.

. . .

"The first couple of days," Charles recounts, "until they got all the body parts that were lying around—people who had jumped from the buildings, people who had jumped from the plane—that was . . ." He pauses, trying not to reanimate the images in his mind. "It was more graphic aboveground than down in the hole."

How many names did they have for it? The hole, the pile, Ground Zero . . . sometimes Charles just called it "9/11"—*I'm going back down to 9/11!*—as if going into a time warp, trying to find trapped survivors and bring them back to the present. During the weeks that the work was actually a rescue, the mission of the responders was crystal clear. But then the focus shifted toward recovery—of things, not people—because the people were gone. Then the rubble was shipped out to be searched through elsewhere, and access to Ground Zero was largely restricted.

But Charles was not done volunteering. Come December, he had started working directly with the victims' families through the efforts of the Red Cross. "That's when I got hooked!" he exclaims. "I became a fool for causes." He distributed supplies and signed over checks at the Family Assistance Center, then located at Pier 94. The help he was providing felt more palpable, face to face with those in need, but so was their sorrow.

By the first week of January 2002, after 117 days of selfless giving, Charles would finally burn out emotionally. On his way back to the offices of the Red Cross, he stopped by the Port Authority to buy a meal. A 9/11 exhibit graced the hallways of the building. Hundreds upon hundreds of photographs of loved ones lost were posted over the walls. He knew they were all gone.

Images from Ground Zero that Charles managed to suppress had come rushing back to his attention: A woman's red purse lay on the floor, her driver's license inside. He wondered who had lost a daughter, and maybe a wife or a mother. What was really getting to him was how the actual people lost to this tragedy were becoming a vivid presence in his mind, as he asked himself, *Who were they? Who had they left behind?*

He just lost it. Tears filled Charles's eyes. It became too personal, and he couldn't keep compartmentalizing. The past long 117 days were composed of so many painful experiences, so many bone-chilling sights and sounds. Tears of deep, raw grief and pain. As the tears flowed, he resolved that he was done for a while: *I can't go there no more,* he thought.

. . .

The last time that Charles cried was a few years back, when his Tana passed away. She had asked Charles to take her to Mount Sinai Medical Center. "She wasn't feeling well," he recalls, but he wasn't worried, since Helen Cook had made it well into her nineties despite her beer-drinking and smoking habits. Sadly, her body shut down just a couple of hours past midnight on that Thanksgiving, right after Charles left her side.

Charles has been separated from his wife for years, yet they remain good friends. She recalls the joyous times the family shared at their Brooklyn home, with Tana joining her great-grandchildren for dinner, then whipping their dad at pinochle over raucous laughter. Carol describes how Charles "loves to joke" and how when playing pinochle, "he tries to psyche the other person out." At times like Thanksgiving, when they all get together, it is clear that Charles is cut from the same cloth as his grandmother. Most important, Carol sums up, "She gave him the love that he needed."

Tana also gave her grandson a lot of confidence navigating the streets of Manhattan. She established her own independence when her family forced her out at the age of sixteen, pregnant with

Charles's father. By the age of seven, Charles was riding the subway on his own from Harlem, picking up his younger brother Dan at school and bringing him along to visit Tana at her apartment smack-dab in the Garment District, where she worked as a seamstress.

She held night jobs at times but also loved to live it up, befriending jazz musicians, including Louis Armstrong, at all the raucous Harlem clubs that didn't charge a cover. On occasion, she'd bring the boy too. Charles would sit by his Tana and sip his Shirley Temple. The child clung to her every expression, doting and attentive.

Charles cried inconsolably at Tana's funeral, as if he had been saving all the tears he hadn't shed for all who had passed before (both of his parents, actually). "She was a friend, not just a grandmother," Charles explains. He did not expect Tana to ever leave his side, even at such an old age, and there was nothing that could have prepared him for that kind of grief.

• • •

Charles has not celebrated Thanksgiving since Tana passed away. However, his coughing fits and chest pains finally forced him, in 2005, to visit the place where he last saw his grandmother. During his first visit, he was tested for possible side effects from his time at Ground Zero. It was only then that he started to seriously commit to his medical treatment.

A friend prompted him to go, suggesting that he might be able to sing again if the doctors cleared up his throat. Charles has a deep voice that is still beautifully mellow but at least an octave lower since 9/11. He can't hold his notes as long as he used to when singing his favorite doo-wop songs or spirituals at church. He is just one of many first responders suffering the effects of the poisonous dust cloud that slowed down their rescue efforts and now threatens to speed up their deaths.

The doctor at Mount Sinai handed Charles a folded sheet of paper. "That has your next appointment written down on it," the doctor said, smiling. Charles took a look. It was a threefold flyer, one of many informative bulletins for first responders consistently printed by Mount Sinai, as the hospital continued to monitor their health. "I'm famous now," Charles joked, wondering why they put that ugly picture of him on the front flap.

Charles's doctors are pleased with his progress so far. They tell him to keep doing whatever he's doing. "I drink vinegar cider sometimes," he explains, a recommendation from an herbalist in Brooklyn. "It cleans my lungs. I still feel like I can't clear my throat, but I've been exercising a lot. I ride bikes, walk eight flights of stairs. So it's working out."

Charles is not alone in his physical struggles post–September 11th; almost all of the rescue workers who pitched in at that time have dealt with long-term difficulties. The debris that remained after the collapse of the towers was "wildly toxic," according to Professor Thomas Cahill, a pollution expert. The debris consisted of more than 2,500 contaminants, many of them carcinogenic. Dr. Larry Norton of Memorial Sloan-Kettering Hospital believes there is a 70 percent illness rate among first responders. In a 2010 study of 5,000 rescue workers, Dr. David J. Prezant found that *all* the workers had impaired lung functions, presenting early on with little improvement with time. Thirty to 40 percent of workers were reporting persistent symptoms and one out of five studied were on "permanent respiratory disability."

The James Zadroga 9/11 Health and Compensation Act, named after a police officer who died of a respiratory disease he contracted during the 9/11 rescue operations, received final Congressional approval on December 22, 2010, and was enacted by President Barack Obama on January 2, 2011. The act will funnel $2.5 billion into a Victims Compensation Fund that will provide aid to first responders and construction workers who were exposed to the World Trade Center dust, as well as some residents in and around Ground Zero. The Zadroga Act also more than quadrupled the funding for health clinics and other programs that screen and treat people for 9/11-related illness. In 2010, these programs received $70 million. They will get $300 million for each of the next five years.

Friends and family continue to question Charles's altruism. If he was aware of the damage to his body, what made him stay so long? "We all chose the way we were gonna go," he says. "But no one need to worry 'bout me." His sickness is his sickness.

. . .

Charles's retirement from recovery efforts was fairly brief. By 2003, he started taking courses in emergency preparedness in order to enhance his already wide range of survival and rescue skills. In

August of 2005, he watched as another disaster unfolded on television: the flooding and devastation left behind by Hurricane Katrina. A young African American child was pleading to the camera for help; his sick grandmother was going to die if she didn't get her medicine. Charles was moved. He knew the time had come once again to leap into action.

In order to receive his assignment from the American Red Cross, Charles had to take a train to D.C., then switch over to the local for Silver Springs, Maryland. There he was told he was being deployed to Montgomery, Alabama. Charles's tinnitus, a debilitating ringing in the ears he developed after a traffic accident, prevented him from traveling by plane. No matter—a group of volunteers who were already planning to drive down offered him a ride.

The nonstop drive extended into the night, and Charles fell asleep in the car. When he awoke, they were in Mississippi. The sun had yet to come up, but even in the darkness he could see what looked to him like a junkyard surrounding them. The "junkyard," he soon realized, was actually the ruins left by the hurricane winds and the floods. The debris stretched for miles and miles.

To make matters worse, Hurricane Rita was now nipping at their heels. The group was forced to stop at a naval base in Gulfport in order to stay safe as the second hurricane in weeks passed over the region. The rain was not heavy, and yet when he went outside, Charles could feel the wet up to his knees. Water pooled quickly in these parts, and he now understood why he saw so many boats caught on tree branches.

Charles had some experience driving large vehicles, as well as operating heavy machinery during his army service, so he was assigned to Emergency Response Vehicle duty. When that didn't work out, he was put in charge of a cargo truck. During the nineties he owned his own van service and provided transportation for performers such as Diana Ross, Jackson Browne, and U2. *If Bono could see me now,* Charles thought.

Charles liked the cargo truck because he could disburse large amounts of food and supplies quickly to as many people as possible. The instructions were clear in terms of what he had to do, yet vague about where he had to do it. He was told to pick an area he wanted to service, drive around to find people in need, then pick up the necessary supplies and deliver them. Repeat. Charles found himself making several trips a day to the warehouse and back out east along the coast, sometimes crossing over to Alabama, where he was originally supposed to be stationed.

One day, as he drove back to the warehouse from a delivery far along Route 9, a woman flagged him down. She had a baby in her arms, pale and puffy like a marshmallow. Charles got out of the cargo truck and asked how he could help. She asked him to come over to her house.

The woman showed Charles that she had no supplies left in the house, not even Similac for the baby. "I don't have much in this truck right now," Charles explained, then added in the most reassuring tone he could muster, "but what I have, I'll give you. Now, you tell all your neighbors who have babies or who need anything else to come meet me here tomorrow at the same time."

The grief in their faces was unbearable. Mothers being unable to care for their babies really got to him. The scene there was worse than 9/11, for him, at least. There was nothing but devastation everywhere he went. Not even the rich had been spared. As he got back on the road toward the warehouse, Charles saw the remnants of a huge estate. Trees were all gone, the fence had been ripped out and lay near a body of water, and there were no houses in sight.

The next day, Charles kept his promise to the woman with the baby, and the woman had brought many of her neighbors with her, all in dire need. Charles gave them all formula and teddy bears. "I've done a lot of things in my life," Charles says with a proud smirk, "but nothing better than that . . . that was my shining hour."

When asked about what Tana would have thought of his volunteer work, Charles says, "She would've expected it."

Grandmother and grandson would often go out fishing in Sheepshead Bay in Brooklyn. In fact, it was a tradition they continued well into her old age, bringing Charles's daughter along as well. Tana was great at it. Whatever they caught on a given day, she brought back home in the evening to distribute to the neighbors. Charles, however, took note of what Tana did when no fish had made it onto their boat. On their way back to Manhattan, she would stop by the market and buy fish.

"Now, don't go telling anyone about this," she'd warn Charles before handing out the fish in the neighborhood. Tana was as proud as she was generous.

Helping others would become a form of healing for Charles. Psychologist Lorne Ladner, Ph.D., asserts that taking care of others is a way of taking care of ourselves. He says, "By developing deep, powerful feelings of compassionate connection with others, we can learn to live meaningful and joyful lives. Only such feelings can help us to learn experientially how to work for meaningful causes and give of ourselves without becoming exhausted or burned out."

Charles would certainly agree. As he shrugs off the idea of receiving anything in return for his help, he says, "We should pay them for the feeling they give us. It's a good feeling, helping people."

• • •

Another New York City summer is ending, and the air this September morning at the park is a bit cooler and drier, making Charles cough repeatedly. He clears his throat and adjusts his Hogwarts baseball cap over his short-cropped, graying afro. He is glad that at least the piercing "sticky-glass" feeling in his lungs isn't there anymore. He reflects, "Lord must have blessed me, 'cause I should be in a box by now. I see so many people sicker than me that spent less time down there."

"Down there" means Ground Zero, where he arrived on September 11, 2001, and stayed for the first 117 days, pouring his soul into the rescue and recovery efforts. C.C., a name familiar to subway riders during his last days as a conductor on the local C line ("C.C.

on the C.C.!" he exclaims), was one of New York City's angels on that day.

With the tenth anniversary almost upon Charles, the words of the Mount Sinai doctors who examined hundreds of first responders like him have made the reality of his failing health feel more imminent. Some of the reports he has read state that inhaling the dust at Ground Zero during the first few weeks after the attacks may have cut his life expectancy by fifteen to twenty years. Charles might not feel old, but he accepts that his time will be up soon. "You come, you go," he nonchalantly tells friends and family.

His casual attitude toward his own death is perhaps possible only because he feels secure that his legacy, the legacy of his grandmother, has been continued in every teddy bear he's pressed into the hands of a forlorn child, every bottle of water he's delivered to an ash-covered emergency worker, and every brick he's cleared from a disaster zone. Charles is a man whose grief is assuaged by giving, whose loss is honored by dedicated service to others.

His service is remarkable and yet not out of the ordinary. Lao Tzu, the celebrated Chinese philosopher and author of the *Tao Te Ching,* teaches that there are four cardinal virtues: reverence for all life, natural sincerity, gentleness, and supportiveness. The last of these, it turns out, is the virtue that releases us from our own pain by allowing us to focus on healing the pain of others.

When grieving a loss in our own lives, sometimes the most powerful action we can take is to forget ourselves for a moment and turn to others—connecting us to all of humanity. Charles has continuously done this, threading the loss of his beloved grandmother to the losses endured by his beloved hometown and his beloved nation. In the process, he has destroyed his body, but his heart is happy. He knows, as Lao Tzu also wrote, that "life and death are one thread, the same line viewed from different sides." Charles ties his fate to the fate of his neighbors, his fellow New Yorkers, his fellow citizens, and so, in a sense, lives forever, just like his Tana.

The Unlikely Activist

Larry Courtney

Larry Courtney excuses himself from his own New Year's Eve party for a moment. He steps onto his large terrace and looks down at tens of thousands of revelers in Times Square, drunkenly swaying arm in arm, blowing kazoos, and squeezing past one another in an effort to get closer to the infamous ball. It will drop shortly. Larry wishes he felt even a fraction of the giddiness of these revelers. He envies their drunken kisses, their sentimental send-off to 2001, the year that's just passed. For him, it can't end soon enough. Though he is fifty-six, he feels one hundred years old.

He takes a deep breath of the cold winter air and exhales, imagining a little bit of grief leaving his body. The lights shine ferociously. He misses his love.

• • •

"I'm in love with you, Gene." The words first came out of Larry's mouth on October 30, 1987. It was, of course, an impetuous thing to say. After all, Larry and Gene had met only a few hours earlier at a Washington, D.C., piano bar. Even offering to give Gene a ride home after their few hours of electric conversation had seemed like a risk, but Larry was filled with a sort of audacious attraction. As he and Gene searched the D.C. streets for Larry's car, he just let it fly.

Eugene, thirty-three, flashed Larry, then forty-two, a "get real" smile and said, "You can't be in love with me. You just met me."

"Just watch," Larry said confidently. When Larry first laid eyes on Gene—this "gorgeous" African American man with a bright smile topped by a dark mustache, and graceful hands—he'd simply known they'd end up together. It was unusual for Larry to be so assertive, but there was something about Gene that made him feel courageous.

• • •

Courage was important to Larry, as it hadn't always come easily. For years, he'd lived the life that he believed he was supposed to live, the life that was expected of him and modeled for him by his parents and grandparents back home in rural Nebraska, all the while ignoring an unalterable truth in his own heart. He'd married and created a family with a woman, although he had long known he was gay.

"It was an act of self-preservation," Larry now explains. Having grown up in a very conservative, religious small town in the late fifties and early sixties, Larry knew from an early age that his gay identity would not be acceptable, so he buried his true sexual orientation and fell into step with his peers—dating, getting married, and having children, just like everybody else.

Larry, his wife, and his three children lived outside Portland, Oregon, and, contrary to what one might expect, had a fairly happy life despite Larry's secret about his true sexual identity. "My wife and I had a number of good years together," Larry explains. "I really loved her even if I wasn't *in* love with her."

They attended a strict Pentecostal Baptist church. At one point, the church organized a protest against an upcoming bill created to ban sexual orientation discrimination in the workplace. Larry did not participate in the march, but he didn't make any public statements against the march either. His betrayal was getting harder and harder to bury.

In 1979, the family moved to Columbia, Maryland—just outside of Washington, D.C.—to fulfill his wife's desire to live near her childhood home. It was in Columbia that their marriage finally unraveled under financial and emotional stress. Larry asked for a divorce.

After the dissolution of their marriage, Larry began going to gay bars in Washington and finally reckoning with his true sexual identity. When he told his ex-wife that he thought he was gay, she admitted that she'd always wondered and offered her loving support, not condemnation. They've maintained a good relationship over the years.

• • •

By 1984, Larry was living in his own place in Columbia, working as an accountant in a gourmet food shop during the day and exploring the vibrant gay scene at night in D.C. He was torn about not living with his three teenaged children, whom he loved more than anything in the world, but he also knew that he would be a better father if he learned how to fully be himself. He was committed to seeing them frequently *and* he was committed to living his whole truth for the first time.

"I finally felt that I was being honest with myself and living the life I should live," Larry explains. "In fact, I felt doubly blessed—I had three children who loved me, which is not something that every gay man can say."

For a few years, Larry was content to explore his new liberation mostly on his own. His life was very full with frequent visits with his kids, an active spiritual and social life, and lots of work. But things shifted when Larry set eyes on Gene. Gene, who taught ballroom dance in his spare time; Gene, who could walk more gracefully in a pair of stilettos than most women could; Gene, who lit up every room.

That beautiful, burnt-orange autumn felt more like spring. "That was it. I was just smitten," Larry remembers. "His eyes, his smile; everything about him was just *life*."

• • •

"I would have to describe my childhood as ideal," Larry says. "We had a very close family." Albion, Nebraska, was a small, rural community, where the two thousand or so residents worked and worshipped with fierce commitment. Larry's father was the quintessential self-sufficient Midwestern man of the house—an electrician, a carpenter, and a handyman. His mother reigned in the domestic realm—making shirts, canning food for the winter, and taking care of Larry and his six siblings. The family was tight-knit and very traditional.

In retrospect, Larry now realizes that they were also short on resources: "We were very poor, but I never thought that." Case in point: Larry was nine years old before his family had their first indoor bathroom.

Larry fondly remembers dinners around his grandparents' table and square dances. "When I was little," he recounts, "the men would go on pheasant hunts on Saturdays in the fall, after the fields had been cut. They would bring back all these pheasants and we'd have feasts."

By six years old, Larry was already noticing that he was more attracted to the boys than to the girls at his elementary school. He didn't think much of it, as he didn't know it was wrong. The church he was raised in never mentioned the politics of sexual orientation, instead focusing on the idea that God loved all of his creations, no exceptions. It was as if homosexuality was so foreign to this congregation that it didn't even warrant mention.

But when fifth grade came around and Larry's family moved to Oregon, he started noticing that the other boys seemed much more interested in girls than he was: "It was at that point that I knew that

I was different," he remembers. "I knew that being gay was being queer, and queer was not good. I kept my feelings to myself."

It was around that same time that Larry first heard his new ministers declare that God hated homosexuals. He puzzled at the contradiction: "That can't be true, because he loves me."

With a child's innocence, Larry reasoned, "God created me the way I am, so why would he hate me? I have always been a child of God." But despite his intuition that the God he'd grown to love would never condemn him for liking boys, he knew that his neighbors and schoolmates would. He didn't want to expose his family to that kind of shame, so he swallowed his secret, determined to create as normal a life as possible.

But as famous writer and gay rights advocate James Baldwin wrote, "An identity would seem to be arrived at by the way in which the person faces and uses his experience." Larry's extraordinary life would not lead him down a normal path. It would inspire his honesty, demand his courage in the face of tragedy, and shape him into an unlikely activist.

. . .

Larry's audacity paid off. By Halloween night of 1987, just one day after meeting for the first time, he and Gene had declared themselves an official couple. Larry took Gene out to dinner to celebrate, then on to the piano bar where they'd first laid eyes on each other. They talked and drank so long that they shut the place down, spilling out onto the street with the lightness of new lovers—oblivious to every-thing but each other.

But their happy oblivion wouldn't last long. As Larry drove toward home, Gene suddenly grew very somber and said, "There is something I need to tell you." Recognizing the seriousness in his tone, Larry pulled over into a church parking lot.

Once they were stopped in the comforting anonymity of the dark lot, Gene said, "I'm HIV positive." He waited a few moments and then added, "I'm going to give you some time to process that," before getting out of the car and standing a few feet away.

Larry, overcome with emotion, leaned his head on the steering wheel and began to cry. He remembers, "I asked God, 'Why? Why, after I've finally found the man I love, are you going to take him away?' I thought it was an immediate death sentence." In fact, the prognosis for HIV-positive Americans has continuously improved thanks to new treatments; according to a federal study published in the January 2010 issue of the *Journal of Acquired Immune Deficiency Syndromes*, average life expectancy after HIV diagnosis increased from ten and a half to twenty-two and a half years from 1996 to 2005.

But Larry, of course, couldn't have known this at the time. Gene got back into the car and they immediately embraced each other, crying into each other's shoulders. Larry knew, just as sure as he had known that he was in love with Gene, that he would never leave him. He didn't care if his partner was faced with a death sentence. He wanted to live by his side. "I'm not letting you go," he told Gene. "I'm taking you home."

. . .

In April 1988, Larry received a job offer in New York City that he could not refuse, as a bookkeeper for Banca IMI, an investment bank. He and Gene decided that, though neither of them had ever even been to New York City before, they would embark on the adventure together. They were head over heels in love and couldn't imagine being apart. Within eight months they lived in Times Square and began exploring the "city of dreams" from its lumines-cent, twenty-four-hour center. "Gene came even more alive," Larry reflects. "He was made for this city."

Gene's personality mirrored the city's: performative, nonstop, and endlessly creative. He loved to go to Broadway shows, squeez-ing Larry's hand as the dancers wound their way across the stage in perfect formation. As the audience spilled out into the streets of the Theater District afterward, Gene looked as if he was lit up from the inside, so inspired by the talent that he'd just seen onstage. They'd make their way back to their apartment, both buzzing with the high of witnessing an inspired performance.

Gene himself worked in office jobs—first in publishing, then in the insurance industry—but he was a huge artistic talent. Larry often quipped, "He could dance like Tina Turner and he had better legs!" By the time he came to New York, he was no longer performing but had long taught dance lessons and performed in various small productions.

Their shared life in the Big Apple was accompanied by a Broadway soundtrack. They loved to buy recordings of their favorite musicals on CD and belt them out as they spent time in their apartment. Gene had a beautiful voice. He drew inspiration from his extensive LP collection—Billie Holiday, Aretha Franklin, and others—and his favorite Broadway shows, *Dreamgirls* and *Les Misérables*.

When they weren't singing and dancing, Larry and Gene were among friends. They loved to have long brunches at their favorite diner, the Viceroy, in Greenwich Village, where Larry would order French toast and Gene would order eggs Benedict, or vice versa. When the pride parade rolled around each June, they got a big group of friends together and marched in honor of their hard-earned liberation. It was wild fun, with people dressed up in costumes, elaborate floats, and, yet again, great music.

Being able to be public as a gay man represented a profound shift for Larry. He was in love and he was living openly, no longer worried about what other people might think. Larry slowly but surely introduced his kids to his new city, new identity, and new partner. Once his eldest son got his driver's license, the kids would all drive up to New York to see Larry and Gene. They took it all in stride, so much so that when Larry sat them down to have the official talk, one son responded with the "well, duh" reaction so familiar to parents who work themselves up to break the news about something delicate with their savvy kids: "Well, yeah, we kind of figured that, Dad."

All three kids immediately took to Gene and appreciated his

generous attention. Not long after meeting them, he bought them each magazine subscriptions based on their unique interests. "They called him the fun stepmother," Larry remembers, laughing.

Larry was even ready to come out to his parents and siblings. In 1990, he sat at the table in his parents' mobile home and told them that Gene was not his roommate, as they'd been led to believe, but his partner. At first, his family was a bit chilly, shocked with the news, confused by his past and all the unanswered questions, but through the process of talking, they came to realize that he was still the same Larry. "It wasn't an easy discussion with my very traditional, down-home family," Larry explains, "but by the end we were all hugging and laughing."

Eventually, all but one brother in his conservative, working-class family would wholeheartedly embrace Larry and Gene. That said, he hadn't yet told them that Gene was African American. When Larry brought Gene to a large family reunion in Oregon shortly thereafter, they were still nervous. It was one thing for Larry's family to accept their love in theory, but to be confronted with it in person, along with Gene's race, might be another story.

"Leave it to Gene to set everyone at ease," Larry remembers. Gene headed straight toward one of Larry's sisters and gave her a big bear hug, exclaiming, "You must be Tootie!" A smile stretched across her face. That's all it took.

From moments like these, Larry knew that he'd found the person who brought out the best in him, helped him loosen up and reach out to others, helped him infuse each and every day with joy and humor. His God, he had always truly believed, didn't care about sexual orientation. His God was more concerned with one's capacity to be transformed by love and love people well. By those standards, Larry knew he was so blessed. As philosopher Ralph Waldo Trine wrote, "A miracle is nothing more or less than this. Anyone who had come into knowledge of his true identity."

. . .

On September 11, 2001, Larry and Gene woke up a bit earlier than usual. It was primary day in New York City, and Gene wanted to make sure he avoided lines at the polls. They drank their coffee in the living room downstairs, and then Gene kissed Larry good-bye. They were looking forward to a home-cooked Southern dinner that night—fried chicken and fried cabbage.

Larry had prepared the meal the night before under Gene's watchful guidance. Though Gene's family moved from North Carolina to Washington, D.C., shortly after he was born, his mother instilled a deep love of Southern food in her boy. A typical Thanksgiving at Gene's house consisted of black-eyed peas, chitlins, collard greens, and headcheese. Larry never could abide by the chitlins or the headcheese but loved to try his hand at other Southern delicacies with Gene's patient help.

It was 8:55 a.m. when Larry arrived at his office on Park Avenue in midtown, walking distance from his apartment. The red message light already blinked incessantly on his office phone. Larry called his voice mail and was greeted with Gene's calm cadence: "Don't worry. The plane hit the other building. We're evacuating and we're okay." Larry had no idea what his beloved was talking about.

That was when Larry noticed his co-workers heading down to the trading floor. A co-worker broke the news: "A plane hit the north World Trade Tower." When Larry pressed her for more details, she admitted that she didn't know much else.

The trading floor monitors were, as usual, blasting a variety of network news broadcasts. Though the forty workers at Banca IMI often huddled around the TVs together, they'd always done so with calculating minds, not concerned hearts. Today was different.

Suddenly, a plane hit the second tower. "Oh my God!" they gasped in unison.

Larry's supervisor came over and gently told him to go back to his desk. "I don't think you need to watch this," she said. Larry was touched that she was concerned, but he was reassured by Gene's message. Gene was okay. He had evacuated early on. He was probably headed home to their apartment at that very moment. Larry called home from his office phone and left a message for Gene directing him to call back when he got home and to let him know that he was okay.

It seemed as if everyone at the office knew people at the World Trade Center. The CEO ordered pizza, feeling compelled to do something, anything, in the face of such shock and confusion. Stricken souls, stunned with the news of the towers collapsing, drew little comfort from numbly eating, roaming around with blank, frightened looks on their faces, calling cell phones of loved ones and friends to no avail.

Wall Street shut down. The tunnels to New Jersey and Long Island were closed. Larry told several co-workers, "If you can't get home, come to my place. Gene and I will make up the sofa bed or put blankets on the floor."

Larry's boss, Melanie, walked home with him. When they arrived at the apartment, they both fully expected Gene to be sitting there, glued to the news like everyone else, but he was not. Everything in the apartment was just as Larry had left it. There was no sign of Gene anywhere.

Larry was surprised and shaky, but far from hopeless. Evelyn, a dear friend, showed up. Melanie, Evelyn, and Larry tried to brainstorm where Gene might be and how they could get in touch with him. As the hours passed with no word from Gene, Larry started to panic. He called the emergency rooms and anyone else he could think of who might know where Gene was.

The night became morning. The next day became the next. Still no word from Gene. The days seemed endless as Larry waited, in vain, for news. Gene's company, Aon, a large insurance company located on the 102nd floor of the South Tower, organized a search party for all of its missing workers, but Gene was not found.

One of Gene's co-workers called to ask if he'd come home. She told Larry that she had seen him helping people onto the elevator and assumed he got out right after that. Larry pictured his dear partner reaching that graceful hand out to help frightened co-workers and friends into the elevator, generous and optimistic as always. "That was just the way he was, other people before him," Larry explains.

After about ten days had gone by, Larry's best friend, Ollie, convinced him to go to the armory to file a missing persons report. Initially, Larry was in total denial and could not admit to himself that Gene might be gone. Plus, he wondered whether the emergency workers would allow him to file a report on behalf of his gay partner or if they would restrict such reports to only heterosexual couples. Larry rarely experienced overt discrimination now that he'd moved to one of the most cosmopolitan cities on earth, but he felt too fragile to contend with any now. He just wanted his Gene to come home. He didn't want to have to explain himself.

The armory was filled with a sea of people and an unmistakable climate of desperation. Larry looked around at the vacant faces and the bodies, stooped with the weight of ready grief. The walls were covered with posters of the missing and tributes to loved ones. Stuffed animals and trinkets were left there, symbols of stubborn hope and impassioned prayer for the return of loved ones.

Larry went up to the first man in official uniform that he found and requested to file a missing persons report. The detective led him to a private table where Larry spoke quietly but honestly about the nature of his relationship with Gene. He broke down in tears as he listened to himself describe his dear love as lost, as if he were watching the whole scene play out from above. The detective immediately responded with kindness and professional assurance that Gene's name and description would become part of the official record. Larry couldn't remember ever being so grateful for someone's kindness.

About four days later, two weeks after the towers first fell, Larry finally accepted that his beloved Gene was really gone. He spoke to several people at Gene's company, all of whom corroborated the first story he'd heard about Gene's last moments—that he'd been helping others into the elevator. No one had seen him after that point. Larry explains, "I had to accept that he was dead. I knew he wasn't coming home. I just gave up hope. That's when I began to grieve."

. . .

For Larry, the loss of his life partner after nearly fourteen years together left him profoundly alone and unbearably empty. He couldn't imagine being without Gene in the years ahead. He had always pictured growing old beside him, having his partner in crime for all of life's adventures, obstacles, and Broadway musicals.

Gene was so full of life. He had a way of putting people—even the most reticent or socially awkward—at immediate ease with a self-effacing joke, a gentle touch on the arm, or an inquisitive question. Though Larry and Gene would often circulate separately at parties, Larry knew he could always glance over and see Gene dazzling someone with his sweet charm. By the end of any and all social gatherings, Gene was everyone's new best friend. As Larry's son Ian describes, "If you looked into Gene's eyes, you could see straight to his soul."

He radiated that energy to those around him, which is why Larry had trouble understanding why his life has been cut so short, at only forty-seven years old: "It just didn't make sense. I could see Eugene at ninety years old organizing ballroom dancing at the nursing home."

As lonely as Larry felt, he did draw strength and comfort from his very close relationships with his family, especially his children and grandchildren. Shortly after Gene's death, Ian drove up from Baltimore with his daughter, Catie. The nine-year-old, who loved coming to New York City and spending time with Grandpa and Gene, wondered out loud at his absence: "Where is Gene?"

"Gene's with his mother, with my father, and with a lot of friends and people that he loves," Larry assured her. Catie didn't mention the subject again during that visit.

The following summer, Ian brought the whole family back to visit. Larry was playing monster and tickling his granddaughter, ever the goofy grandpa, when Catie began to cry and sobbed, "I miss Gene."

"It was so funny to see this ten-year-old having that much emotion about this man that she just knew as my partner," Larry explains. "We spent about half an hour just holding each other, and crying, and talking, and then we kinda got through it."

Larry was adept at getting through isolated moments like these, but the grief—writ large—felt like it lasted forever. It was too hard for Larry to accept that Gene was gone. Dr. Leeat Granek, head of the Grief and Loss Project, a cross-national consortium on the study of grief and loss in Canada and the United States, explains, "Grief and loss are normal, expected and constant."

Sitting with the grief, as Larry did, is a necessary part of getting to good feelings again. Dr. Granek elaborates: "There is often an attempt to banish the negative feelings because they feel so bad, and while that is understandable in the moment, what happens when you cut out one end of the emotional spectrum—sadness—is that you also inadvertently cut out the other end—joy. We have to fully feel all of our emotions in order to alchemize them into something generative."

Larry kept replaying the day in his mind: Gene had left a reassuring message early in the day saying he and his co-workers were evacuating, but what happened after that? Not knowing the details of that day, of Gene's last moment, drove him crazy—and knowing that he would never really know left him restless. He could not avoid feeling anger as he wondered what had prevented Gene's escape.

But the anger was softened by his knowledge that Gene had been helping people out the day that he died. Larry flashed back to their most recent family reunion, in April 2001, when he had fallen ill from severe viral pneumonia. Gene refused to leave his side in the hospital, calling in sick to work and requesting that the nurses bring in a cot so he could sleep next to wheezing Larry. Of course, one would expect that kind of care from a loving partner, but Larry knew that Gene didn't reserve his care just for his nearest and dearest. Gene felt a responsibility to reach out to perfect strangers with similar tenderness. As much as Larry grieved losing him, he was also proud that his partner had died being his generous, courageous self.

In early October of 2001, Larry headed to the Family Assistance

Center at Pier 94 to file for Eugene's death certificate. Scores of people who had lost a loved one in the terrorist attacks on the World Trade towers made their way along the West Side Highway to the vast, aluminum-sided building on Pier 94. Larry made his way past the uninviting exterior and into the main hall and was stunned to find the most beautifully decorated space he could have imagined for grieving families. "They carpeted the whole pier in soft blues," he describes. "It was like being in heaven, surrounded by angels. These people had come from all over the country as volunteers."

One such volunteer was assigned to usher Larry around and offer him food and drink. He was taken first to a lawyer, who filed the affidavit, and then to several other stations, including the Red Cross and the Crime Victims Board. Larry couldn't believe that something he'd dreaded so passionately had turned out to be such a gentle experience, just like his day at the armory. It was still painful, but the kindness of others was a powerful balm.

That evening, Larry decided to treat himself to dinner at his and Gene's favorite restaurant, a tribute to having gotten through such a difficult day with such sweet assistance. The maître d' recognized him instantly and asked, puzzled, "Just you?"

"Yes, I've been at the family center all day," replied Larry. All New Yorkers at that time knew what the family center was.

"Did you lose someone?"

"Eugene," Larry answered as tears started to well up in his eyes. They hugged each other for a very long moment.

• • •

After all the arrangements pertaining to Gene's death, Larry wanted to do something to honor his life. In October of 2001, he invited friends and family to a big celebration of Eugene Clark's indomitable spirit.

As guests started arriving at noon, Larry stayed at the top of the stairs of his duplex, giving people huge Gene-like greetings and hugs as they came up—a loving tribute to Gene's warmth and life-of-the-party presence. Larry also bought an extravagant arrangement of orchids that leaned, long and thin, just like Gene, over all the beautiful food that his guests brought.

Although the afternoon was a blur for Larry, he still has the guestbook from the party, signed by ninety-six people. He also has the transcripts of hundreds of messages left on his voice mail in honor of Gene, dating back to 9/11. These are the artifacts he returns to when he wants to remember how loved his dear partner really was.

• • •

Larry stayed in New York for a couple of years following Gene's death. He worked hard, spent lots of time with friends, and cooked up plans for a West Coast homecoming with his children, who also had their hearts set on living closer together. (They either already lived on the West Coast or planned to relocate there.) But no matter how much Larry packed into his schedule, no matter how many wonderful friends he managed to spend time with, the Big Apple wasn't the same without Gene. "I was lonely, even when I was busy," Larry remembers.

Larry's loss left him lonesome, to be sure, but it also provided him with an opportunity to honor Gene's outspoken legacy. Among the heaps of mail that Larry received after Gene's death, a letter from Cambridge Insurance caught his eye. It notified him about an upcoming workers' compensation hearing. Larry had not even considered filing for workers' compensation, believing that his homosexual relationship, although technically a domestic partnership recognized by the state of New York, would not qualify him for spousal benefits. But as he heard the stories of other widows and widowers filing claims, he began to grow uncomfortable with his assumption. Why shouldn't he be afforded the same rights as heterosexual people in his same situation? Gene wouldn't have been meek in a situation like this. He would have said something. Larry decided to go for it.

At the first hearing Larry went to, the insurance agent told him that he didn't have any standing because he was not Gene's legal spouse. The judge at the hearing advised him to get a lawyer who could fight for his rights to compensation. The Lambda Legal Defense and Education Fund had been reviewing the cases of more than twenty gay partners of victims of the September 11, 2001, terrorist attacks and had found that the law did not define "spouse" by the existence of a marriage certificate. Larry became one of Lambda's pro bono clients, and together they took their fight to Albany.

The lawyer advised Larry to gather letters from his friends and family, confirming that Larry and Gene had been a long-standing couple. But even with all the strong support (friends responded generously), the judge continued to request additional hearings. Larry's determination did not wane. At the end of the fourth hearing, the state of New York finally not only ruled in Larry's personal favor but also instituted a public law that recognizes surviving domestic partners' right to workers' comp for those lost in the attacks of September 11th. Larry is now set to receive four hundred dollars a week for the rest of his life.

Larry's case became big national news. He was interviewed by Katie Couric and Anderson Cooper. Though he was nervous to be featured on such big media outlets, he drew on a strength born of his relationship with Gene. "He would be proud!" Larry exclaims.

. . .

In March of 2004, Larry made the final leap to a new life.

The house he found in San Jose, California, was small but quaint. It was a far cry from the dream house Larry has been drafting sketches of since he was a child, but it was a peaceful home, a place where Larry could get away from the New York hustle and heal.

But he didn't leave New York completely behind. Somehow, he managed to reconfigure his new place with the same layout as his New York apartment—a little piece of his life with Gene that he held on to. Additionally, he hung a big portrait of Gene in the living room so he could walk by and see his smiling face every day. The sting began to soften. He explains, "I see the face of a friend I can just talk to. It doesn't bring back heart-wrenching grief anymore."

San Jose was serene and quiet, although very much a city, and a mere forty-five minutes from lively San Francisco. Larry was also just twenty-five minutes from the beach, where the roaring majesty of the Pacific Ocean had a calming effect for him.

Perhaps most surprising to Larry was the fact that he now had a roommate—one of his daughter's friends. After getting used to living alone for the first few years after Gene's death, he was amenable to the company, especially that of someone so respectful and unobtrusive as Davey—a Hawaiian who had two sweet dogs and made a great lunch partner. Before long, Davey's partner moved in, and the three of them happily coexisted for a short time before the two younger men decided to return to Davey's tropical home. Larry's daughter helped him find a great apartment of his own, in the comforting shade of palm trees.

Larry became an active member of his local congregation of the United Church of Christ, a large one at almost four hundred members, in 2006. The fifth-anniversary ceremony at Ground Zero had been a tremendous turning point in his life. Laying down a rose for Gene that day had taken on a new meaning: It was a type of letting go that had not been previously possible for Larry. He had come to the following realization: "I am a whole person, but I don't want to operate in a vacuum. I think I operate better in a community, with other people."

He had been mindful of finding what is called an Open and Affirming church. According to the UCC Coalition for LGBT Concerns' website, this designation stands for "congregations, campus ministries, and other bodies in the United Church of Christ which make public statements of welcome into their full life and ministry to persons of all sexual orientations, gender identities, and gender expressions."

Larry had been very active in various church communities throughout his life, but in San Jose, he was happy to find a place where he could develop his spirituality and not have to defend his sexual orientation. Larry explains, "I'm not out to convert anybody, but to me, the love of my creator is the most important and constant thing in my life, so I just feel that that's the calling. I need to share this with others. If I can help one person release the hurt and help them realize they are loved and cared for, that's enough."

. . .

During one of his trips back to New York City to honor Gene at Ground Zero, Larry experienced a chance happening that he believes might have been destined.

After the annual memorial ceremony, he took the subway to the hotel, hoping to change his clothes before meeting up with friends for dinner. He decided to stop by the bar for a drink before taking the elevator up to his room.

A few minutes later, a woman approached Larry and sat down on the stool next to him. She pointed at the ribbon he was wearing on his shirt, which was actually a victim's family badge. "So of course," Larry recounts, "she asked me who I had lost at the World Trade Center. And I told her."

"How weird!" the woman replied. "I used to work at Aon. I left in 2000. I knew so many people there." Aon lost three hundred people in the attacks. The woman proceeded to name several of her former co-workers. Larry recognized many of them. Eugene's name was familiar to her as well, so she asked what he looked like.

"He was a gorgeous black man with the most beautiful smile," Larry answered, a smile spreading across his face.

Her jaw dropped. "I saw his poster . . . and I saw you on TV. I knew I recognized you from somewhere!" the woman exclaimed. "Thank you so much for fighting for our rights. I'm gay too, and that might be a fight I won't have to take on because of you."

Larry felt as if Gene had played some role in sending this grateful woman, a reminder that his bravery in the face of loss hadn't been just for his own personal benefit.

• • •

Today Larry still misses New York: the vibrant Greenwich Village nightlife, the pageantry of opening night for a Broadway musical, the convenience of taking the subway everywhere. And he is keenly aware of how much he still misses Gene. He thinks about him every single day, without fail. "I'm not sure you ever finish the grief process," Larry reflects. "My faith tells me he's safe now and that someday I will be there too. Having that faith has gotten me through a lot of days."

Rabbi Michael Paley, scholar in residence at the United Jewish Appeal Federation in New York, explains that spiritual belief "allows one to have access to other worlds, allows us to see possible in the impossible." Faith that he will be reunited with Gene is a comforting thought to Larry in difficult times.

Although Larry religiously returns to Manhattan to honor Gene each September, he has settled into the more tranquil pace of his life in San Jose—surrounded by lots of family and friends. He continues to be an active member of his church, volunteering twice a week in the office, playing in the bell choir, and helping out with LGBT-related ministries.

Ten years later, Larry still doesn't feel the push to find a new romantic love, only to deepen his spiritual connection. He explains, "I believe in a creator, and my journey is to figure out what that higher power wants from me and what I can give back."

Gene, though gone, has continued to be a major source of energy in Larry's life. He is still there in spirit, pushing Larry forward in his activism, giving him confidence to be more outgoing, reminding him of all the joy to be had in living.

Larry thinks of Gene in his last moments, extending a hand to frightened co-workers, and feels compelled to bring the same level of brave altruism to his own daily life. Supported by his continued relationship with Gene and his everlasting relationship with God, he keeps on. Larry summarizes: "You have to plug yourself into the source if your life is going to shine."

Larry, like so many of those who lost loved ones on September 11, carries Gene with him in a truly substantive way. He's not just a faint presence or a nostalgic memory, but an active and ongoing influence on who Larry is, what choices he makes, and how he sees the world.

Freud believed that the end of mourning is marked by what he called "interiorization"—the total inward acceptance that a person's death transforms that person into only a memory, only a past-tense preoccupation. French philosopher Jacques Derrida offers a different perspective: "Upon the death of the other we are given to memory, and thus to interiorization, since the other, outside us, is now nothing. And with the dark light of this nothing, we learn that the other resists the closure of our interiorizing memory." In other words, as long as we continue to be in dialogue with those we've loved and lost, as long as we make choices influenced by what we think they might recommend, or try on their worldview from time to time, they remain, in a sense, "alive" for us.

Though experts long believed that such a continued relationship might be harmful, preventing the bereaved from truly moving on, new research and evolved wisdom indicates that many of the healthiest and happiest mourners are those who figure out a way to continue to feel connected to those they've lost. As Larry demonstrates, the more we embrace the nuanced truth—that death doesn't actually kill a bond, but alters it—the more gracefully we heal.

A Life Built on Brotherhood

Tim Brown

Tim Brown scanned the chaos in the lobby of Tower 1, the North Tower, assessing the situation—the abandoned newsstands, the people in business suits and janitorial garb bottlenecking at the top of escalators as they headed toward the exits with naked fear on their faces. He went downstairs to the fire command post and discovered a black-and-yellow-striped sea of New York City firefighters—thirty or so in all.

Tim quickly spotted his mentor and best friend, Terry Hatton, suited up and ready to head higher in the flaming tower. Even in this cacophony, Terry was hard to miss; at six foot four barefoot, and nearly six foot eight with his gear on, he was a mountain of a man, one of the most respected leaders in the most respected fire department in the country. Tim and Terry had met through work, but their friendship extended far beyond the brick walls of the firehouse. They drank together (Tim could hold his liquor far better than Terry), talked about their dreams and frustrations, and celebrated Terry's marriage to salt-of-the-earth Beth when the happy day came. If they had been actual brothers, Terry would have been the older one.

Tim, in fact, was a man with many brothers—three biological and many, many picked up along the way. One might describe his whole life as being built on a foundational belief in the importance of brotherhood—that old-world value of being there for the man who would, in turn, be there for you. It was an idea that gave him great comfort, an idea that guided his entire life.

As Tim approached, Terry and he locked eyes. Finally face to face, they gave each other a knowing look and a hearty hug, made even heavier by the force of Terry's gear. "Might be the last time I see you, brother," Terry told Tim. "I love you, man."

Prior to the attacks on the World Trade Center in 2001, Tim accepted an assignment from the FDNY to serve in the New York City Office of Emergency Management (OEM), established in 1996. The OEM was located in what many called "the bunker" in 7 World Trade Center. As a supervisor of field operations, Tim's responsibilities that day were to coordinate emergency response in the field and communicate the conditions back to the state-of-the art communications center. This could mean anything, including working with the FDNY fire chief, the Port Authority, Con Edison, and the mayor.

From the moment the lights flashed off and on again at 8:46 a.m., Tim put down his newspaper, abandoned his breakfast, and jumped into action. After making sure that the watch command was up and running on the twenty-third floor, and grabbing his three portable radios, he went to assess the situation on the ground—"already like a war zone," as he describes it—from three sides, a maneuver that was a holdover from his firefighter training. He went to the lobby command post in Tower 1 to assist the incident commander but was quickly redirected to the Tower 2 command post when the second plane hit. After trying to help a group of people who were trapped in a burning elevator car, Tim needed to get the paramedics into the lobby to start removing the injured.

When Tim was returning to the Tower 2 lobby with the paramedics, they suddenly heard an unmistakable sound—the creaking of 1,172 feet of load-bearing perimeter steel columns. He explains, "There has never been anything more clear to me in my life than what that sound was. I knew instantly that the building was collapsing. The sound was deafening and it was progressive. You could actually hear each floor collapse."

Tim ran toward the Marriott in 3 World Trade Center for cover, but just as he went in, the lights went out and the wind picked up to what scientists now believe was 185 miles per hour. "I couldn't see anything. I couldn't hear anything," Tim remembers.

He knew he'd be killed if he went outside, where steel was crashing down onto the street, so he wrapped his arms around a nearby column in the Marriott and held on for dear life. Tim remembers, "When the buildings were falling down on top of me, I could only think of two things: I want to quit my job, because it's not worth it, and I want to be with my brother Chris."

Chris Brown, meanwhile, was in Providence, Rhode Island, relieved to have his first day off from the firehouse in weeks, until he heard what was going on in New York and was flooded with thoughts of his brother Tim inside the towers. He watched the play-by-plays on television and prayed that his phone would ring and that his brother's voice would be on the line.

Tim's helmet blew off. The noise was unbearable. The dust and debris hit him in the face at piercing speed. He was waiting to get crushed. It felt like years went by in those eight fateful seconds. It would turn out that when Tower 2 collapsed, it *did* fall on the hotel and Tower 3, except for one tiny section where Tim clung to his column and waited to die.

Tim describes the calm that followed: "The collapse stopped. The wind stopped. The noise stopped. You couldn't see anything. It was an eerie silence for a minute or two. Nobody was stirring. Nobody was moving. Everyone was in shock. Everyone was trying to move their parts to see if they still worked."

Tim managed to follow a shaft of light to find his way out of what was left of the Marriott lobby and began scaling rubble—sometimes three and four stories high. "I was in flight mode at that point," he remembers. "I just wanted to get as far away as possible."

Responses like Tim's are well documented by psychologists. Our fight-or-flight instinct, as it's popularly known, was first noted by neurologist Walter Cannon in 1929 while observing the ways in which animals confronted threatening situations. Now we understand that both animals and humans have diverse responses to threats—everything from throwing a punch willy-nilly to freezing up so as to observe every detail of the perilous situation before making a decision about what to do next. In almost all cases, however, the physiological effects are similar: When we perceive danger, hormones are released via a signaling process in our brains that preps our bodies for fight, flight, or freeze. Our hearts beat faster, our lungs take in more oxygen, and our digestion slows down. It's a rapid and reliable process that pushes us to take self-protective action, even before we are aware of what's really going on.

Tim was able to put a bit of distance between himself and the carnage, take a deep breath, and try to reason out the most important next steps. Shortly thereafter, he heard that same foreboding creak again. "I saw the top of Tower One lean over and then disappear," he recounts somberly. "I knew Terry was in there."

Terry Hatton, captain of Rescue 1, died, along with 342 other firefighters who headed high into the burning towers on September 11, 2001. Tim personally knew 93 of them.

• • •

Tim grew up in suburban Connecticut, where most of the fathers were more akin to Ward Cleaver than to Clark Kent. The insurance business was a big employer among the families in Tim's cohesive, middle-class neighborhood, but his father was actually a research scientist for United Technologies, a defense contractor. It often felt as if his little town was insulated from the cultural shifts going on in the late sixties; women were still stay-at-home moms, sometimes frustrated mothers, and men were suited, mostly absent fathers.

Even as a child, Tim was surrounded by a brotherhood. He was one of five kids, with only one girl in the mix. He and his brother Chris would watch the television police drama *Adam-12,* and then pretend they were cops staking out the perimeter and dodging danger among the broken-down cars in the backyard. Their true heroes were paramedics Johnny Gage and Roy DeSoto from another hit drama of the early seventies, *Emergency!* which mixed action-adventure and medical drama. They were Boy Scouts together in Troop 341.

While he loved the camaraderie of having so many brothers, by high school he was feeling undeniably lost. He didn't like school, particularly because he didn't like to be told what to do. Tim's struggle with authority was seeded in those early days of rebelling against his teachers and school administrators.

He'd rather be playing ice hockey at Mill Pond down by the tracks across from his house or smoking cigars in the fort that he and his boys built. From the age of about twelve until seventeen, when Tim's parents finally got divorced, the family was often in turmoil—fights, financial woes, and disappointment after disappointment. Tim longed for a different kind of life from the unhappy suburban one he had known. He longed for a vocation with more adrenaline than life insurance policies or lab research. He wanted to feel like he really mattered.

Jay, a childhood friend, was the first one who introduced Tim to the excitement of chasing fires. They would sit in Jay's car, talking, and listening to the squawk of the radio scanner. When the dispatcher announced that a fire had broken out, it was like Jay and Tim had won the jackpot. They'd start up the engine and hightail it toward the site, prepared to watch the real heroes fight the flames. Before long, they became junior firemen together. Tim reflects, "That steered me away from trouble and gave me a true passion to be a fireman. I enjoyed the freedom of going into a fire and coming out triumphant."

Being a firefighter comes with the reward of brotherhood, but also the risk of great harm. It is a dangerous profession that requires sacrifice, as reflected in the sacred oath of those who fight fires for a living:

I PROMISE CONCERN FOR OTHERS. A WILLINGNESS TO HELP ALL THOSE IN NEED. I PROMISE COURAGE— COURAGE TO FACE AND CONQUER MY FEARS. COUR- AGE TO SHARE AND ENDURE THE ORDEAL OF THOSE WHO NEED ME. I PROMISE STRENGTH—STRENGTH OF HEART TO BEAR WHATEVER BURDENS MIGHT BE PLACED UPON ME. STRENGTH OF BODY TO DELIVER

TO SAFETY ALL THOSE PLACED WITHIN MY CARE. I PROMISE THE WISDOM TO LEAD, THE COMPASSION TO COMFORT, AND THE LOVE TO SERVE UNSELFISHLY WHENEVER I AM CALLED.

The burden of death is the ultimate sacrifice of firefighters and their families everywhere—the great price that comes with wearing the uniform, with feeling that deep sense of purpose, with helping people. Tim explains, "They all did something for us that is bigger than we even realize now. Over time we will see what they did for us."

For Tim, the sacrifice is not just noble or abstract. It is personal: "It's hard when it's your friends that did that. I'm very proud of them. I don't know that a lot of people realize the gravity of what happened. It's something that will be told over time, historically, by our children's children."

In the meantime, Tim and his brother Chris pitched in with the recovery effort. Together, united by a sense of duty and deep integrity, they spent the first four months following the September 11th attacks working eighteen-plus-hour days at Ground Zero and at the forward command post in the OEM. They—like Brian and Charles and so many other generous and inexhaustible souls—did what needed to be done, whether that was coordinating communication between city agencies, securing necessary gear and tools for the rescue and recovery workers, or rolling up their own sleeves and digging through the rubble.

Tim found new purpose doing the heavy lifting at Ground Zero, but he also found meaning in doing the little things that he believes Terry would have done had he lived. "People don't remember that someone has to take the garbage out, cut the lawn, hang the mirror, move the furniture, and give a hug," Tim explains. He has vowed to step in where his friends left off, to be a helping hand and an emotional support to his friends' grieving widows, mothers, and fathers as much as he can.

Tim listens to the sound of his paint roller against the naked wall—up and down, up and down, in a soothing rhythm—as he paints the walls of baby Terri's bedroom pansy pink. Just ten days after the attacks, Beth found out that she was pregnant with her husband Terry's child—their first and only. Tears roll down Tim's cheeks, even though it feels good to help out. It's a relief to focus on the mundane—not the loss of ninety-three personal friends, but the installation of a light fixture soft enough that it won't hurt a baby's newborn eyes. In the face of such vast and profound loss, Tim craves the simple and the mindless, the sound of that paint roller, the space to let tears come without self-consciousness.

Those quiet moments of grief are soon crowded out by big moves that Tim feels he must make in order to play his part in the nation's recovery. When Secretary Tommy Thompson of the U.S. Department of Health and Human Services calls in July of 2002 and asks for Tim's help coordinating the response to anthrax, he is convinced that it is the next step in his predetermined path. He explains, "My fate, although I didn't realize it, is to go to Washington and work on a different scale. We can share our experiences with the whole country, instead of just New York City. We can make things better."

Before long, Tim's work is collapsed into the Department of Homeland Security, which was formed in 2003 from a restructuring of preexisting federal agencies—the biggest government reorganization in American history. Its mission is to protect America from future terrorist attacks, as well as respond when natural disasters strike. It is now the third largest Cabinet department, with more than two hundred thousand employees and a $50 billion average annual budget.

When Tim signed on, DHS was still in its early stages, grappling to figure out the most effective structures and systems to prevent and prepare for future attacks and emergencies. Tim dove into his work—relieved at the distraction of twelve-hour days, seven days a week. Underneath the demands of work, however, he felt a sadness more profound than any he had ever known. He was plagued by a sense of unceasing loneliness.

His brother Chris left his own family behind to move down to Washington, D.C., hoping to give his mourning brother some companionship, at least temporarily. Tim remembers those days fondly: "We worked together, had dinner together, had a cigar together, then we'd go to sleep, get up, and do it all again. I will love my brother forever for that."

But eventually Chris would have to go back to Providence to be near his children, who had needs of their own. Without the salve of brotherhood, Tim's loneliness calcified. His sense that he was not, as he'd hoped, in the right place, doing the right thing, began to gnaw at him daily. He remembered the crystal-clear thought that had echoed in his brain as he clung to that column as the world crashed down around him: "By being separate from him I broke the promise that I made to myself—that if I lived, I would be near my brother for the rest of my life."

On the evening of February 20, 2003, fate stepped in once again. Chris called Tim at about midnight and told him to turn on the television. Tim saw the first breaking news reports about a deadly nightclub fire in West Warwick, Rhode Island. It appeared to be very bad.

Twenty hours later, Tim was there, working with emergency personnel and city and state health officials, at the request of Secretary Thompson. Twenty-four hours after that, Tim had stepped into a role advising Governor Donald L. Carcieri, whose team had been in office for only thirty days, on a range of emergency issues. They would go on to create the Disaster Mortuary Operational Response Team, identifying ninety-six badly burned bodies in just three days and returning their remains to their loved ones.

The fire began in that nightclub when one of the night's acts used pyrotechnics that ignited flammable sound-insulation foam on the walls and ceilings around the stage. Within just five and half minutes, the whole club was engulfed in flames, the heavy smoke obscuring the exits and making it difficult for people to find their way to safety. More than 230 people were injured and 100 were killed, making it the fourth-deadliest nightclub fire in American history.

Tim's temporary detail to Rhode Island would eventually lead to a full-time position helping the governor coordinate all the state's public safety agencies. He moved to Providence, where he could be near his brother Chris once again and continue his firefighter brothers' legacies of assisting civilians in emergencies.

On September 8, 2003, Tim and his brother Chris stood together among a sea of thousands of other brave men and women in Bergen Beach, Brooklyn, at the very last funeral for a firefighter killed on September 11. The wake and church service for Mike Ragusa, age twenty-nine at the time of his death, were over, and everyone stood outside. Helicopters flew overhead in the clear blue sky. People sniffled quietly, overcome with the emotion of finally being at the end of the official mourning rituals. The firefighters held formation, held their breath, held their pain.

The pipe band marched by while the trumpeters played taps for the 343rd firefighter since September 11, 2001. Tim explains, "The pipe band made a promise that they would not play a happy song until the last fireman was buried. They came back the opposite way and played two of the happiest songs that they knew. As they went by, the whole line of five thousand firemen gave them a standing ovation for, like, ten minutes.

"It was kind of closure for us, you know," he goes on. "Especially for the band. I don't know if you can imagine playing these sad dirges more than 343 times. It was a good sign for us, time to move forward and try and start seeing the happy things in life again."

Being in Rhode Island had its perks. Tim took daily walks by the water, reflecting on his life and its many twists and turns. He had a new hero in Governor Carcieri—"After so many bad things," Tim describes, "he represents honesty." Tim was also regularly seeing a counselor, whom he instantly trusted, as she had also seen his brother. And best of all, he was able to see Chris regularly. "We yakety-yak like two old washwomen," Tim jokes. "When I'm with him, that's all I need. I don't need anything else in my life. He fulfills me."

Tim also craved a deeper, more consistent relationship with the families that his friends in New York left behind. "It's sometimes hard for us to have a relationship," he explains. "Some of these folks who were so horribly impacted—[they] need to leave that whole life behind. That's the only way they can survive. Maybe these folks don't really need me in their lives anymore. It's not out of a lack of love, but out of pain."

Terry's wife, Beth, moved to Long Island to live a quieter, easier life. Baby Terri, not such a baby any longer, thrived in elementary school. Tim dreams of taking her down to Ground Zero when the Freedom Tower is finally finished, pointing to the top of the building way up in the sky, and telling her that this is her daddy's legacy.

Tim needed to feel needed. He worked excessively at his new job in Rhode Island, trying to stave off the dark thoughts and deep sadness by spending hours and hours at his desk. Some days were good. He felt as if he was really building support for a more comprehensive emergency plan for Rhode Island, really making a difference in people's lives. Some days were bad. He would stare at his computer screen and a dead blankness would fill his mind. At these moments, he felt a fatigue unlike anything he'd ever experienced, as if his very soul were tired. "Sometimes I'll just sit there and cry quietly," Tim explains.

It wasn't long before Tim realized that Rhode Island was yet another place he was retreating to, to hide from his past. The "blues"—as Tim called the feelings of depression that plagued him—continued. Tim realized he needed to make a big change. "I've been running for three years," he admits. "My soul has been in turmoil."

On July 12, 2004, Tim retired, determined to keep growing his roots in Rhode Island without the distraction of a demanding job and with the comfort of a small pension. He devoted his full attention to the website he cofounded with his brother in 1999, TheBravest .com, which celebrates and honors firefighters. He sipped tea and read the morning newspaper front to back, took long walks around Providence, and continued to see his counselor, trying to unpack all the pain and loss he'd been storing up over the past three years of feverish work.

Much of Tim's post-9/11 life was spent trying to figure out how to be the keeper of his firefighting brothers' legacies. Sometimes he questioned whether he did the right thing that day, but he quickly corrected his doubts with the surety of God's plan: "Of course I feel horribly guilty. I wish I could have stood there and held the towers up. But God has something else in store for me. The only way I can help people is to be alive to do it."

After a couple of listless years in Providence, Tim moved back to New York in 2005. "It's better for my life to be here and better for my brother's [Chris's] life for me to be here," Tim explains. "He's got some challenges right now with his kids, work, and the website. He didn't need to have a third child around. He wanted to spend time with me, but it was a burden."

Back in New York—among the skyscrapers and smoke, the constant ambulance sirens and the familiar buzz of unending activity—Tim thought of his lost friends all the time. Their ghosts were all around—at the pub where Terry and Tim used to have a pint, in every firehouse he passed, and of course, at Ground Zero itself. Tim ached for the familiar pace of emergency-responder work. Though he knew that his healing was facilitated by slowing down, he was sick of all the downtime. He was ready to work again.

In 2006, he took a job with Solutions America, the political action committee for Rudy Giuliani, who would make a run for president in 2008. Building on Giuliani's reputation as rising to the occasion amid the devastation on September 11, Tim envisioned running a program for first responders in his name, but for a time he was simply charged with traveling around and spreading Giuliani's message. He explains, "It's very deep and very emotional to be a part of this, to be able to go throughout the country and meet these people and hear their stories about how they came to help us, and be able to share my stories with them." Shaping the ongoing narrative of September 11th, and listening to the way it had shaped others, was another facet of Tim's healing.

In large part, he took the job because he believed it was something his lost friends would respect: "My friends were carrying the torch and now they're gone, and it's time for me to carry the torch a bit. In their honor, in their families' honor, but even more to protect people here. I believe in the mayor so strongly. I think he's a good man. I think he's a great leader."

The voters disagreed. In January of 2008, following a debilitating defeat in the Florida primaries, Giuliani announced that he was dropping out of the race and endorsing John McCain, the former POW, whom Giuliani believed "could be trusted in times of crisis." He went on, "Obviously, I thought I was that person. The voters made another choice."

Tim was disappointed. This time, it wasn't so much a fallen leader that he was mourning, but his own idealism. Politics had proven to be, in Tim's words, "a dirty, dirty game." He felt that it was his duty to carry on the legacies of his fallen brothers, and yet he struggled to find the most effective, most noble way to do so. He'd tried to stay close to their widows and children, but in some ways he was too potent a reminder of the men that they had lost. Many of them were trying to move on, which meant letting some of their past relationships languish. He'd given back at the national and state levels, but without being connected to the site where his friends had perished, it didn't quite fulfill him. It was noble, to be sure, but not a direct enough expression of his loyalty. His relationship with his own brother Chris, while still paramount, was no substitute for the loss of so many other friends and mentors, most especially Terry.

In many ways, it was as if a simpler time had passed, and there was nothing he could do to get it back. Tim longed to return to the singular focus of emergency work, the clear mission of helping people in crisis, the burly arms of a brotherhood, but his life would never be so straightforward again. It had been colored by profound loss, the complexity of grief, the disappointment that inevitably follows high hopes for resolution.

It was as if Tim's very DNA had been altered by the losses he experienced. Thrity Umrigar, an Indian novelist, writes:

> Perhaps time doesn't heal wounds at all, perhaps that is the biggest lie of them all, and instead what happens is that each wound penetrates the body deeper and deeper until one day you find that the sheer geography of your bones— the angle of your head, the jutting of your hips, the sharpness of your shoulders, as well as the luster of your eyes, the texture of your skin, the openness of your smile—has collapsed under the weight of your grief.

Indeed, Tim felt the ten-ton burden, not just of his own sadness, but of the responsibility of carrying on his brothers' legacy, as surely as he did the ache in his back and the beating of his own heart. He had been forever and inextricably altered.

Though Tim had literally attempted to work through his grief, as Freud might have advised him, it would prove too stubborn, too unpredictable. Tim was faced, and is still facing, the nonlinear project of healing and paying homage to the emergency workers who died on September 11, not just an abstract group to him, a nameless crowd of yellow and black, but ninety-three people whose names, faces, and stories he knows personally.

Mourning of that magnitude is most certainly not executed in five distinct stages, as Kübler-Ross suggested. In fact, its nature—in many senses—is the exact opposite of Tim's training. There is no preparedness plan possible, no step-by-step system to follow, no way to keep one's heart safe from the flames of sudden loss. It just is. And nothing could be harder to process for a man who has dedicated his life to preventing what danger may come.

Digging Out of the Darkness

Joe Keenan

A couple of guys put down their rakes and came running back from the field, abandoning the pile of debris they were inspecting. As they approach the wind tent, with their goggles and white Tyvek suits glimmering against the gray landscape, they look like astronauts exploring an alien planet. The image is complete when they proudly hold up a battered, ashen American flag.

"Look what we found here!" one of the guys exclaims. He asks Detective Sergeant Joseph "Joe" Keenan about taking a picture with the flag.

"Guys, we have a procedure here," Joe reminds them. Joe, soft-spoken but strong, in his early fifties, sometimes feels like a teacher who has to keep reminding his students how to behave, but he's glad that the workers respect his authority.

...

It is another wintry morning at Fresh Kills. For more than six months now, most of the wreckage from the World Trade Center has been lying all around Joe at this former landfill, a twenty-one-mile drive from Lower Manhattan. He is one of the supervisors of a recovery effort that includes more than a thousand workers, among them NYPD officers, FBI agents, and sanitation workers.

Joe's job is undeniably grim. On any given day, his team of detectives finds yet another fingernail or sliver of bone as they inspect a load of debris. These sometimes very delicate remains are saved and cataloged in hopes that they might bring comfort, however inadequate, to a grieving family member, or insight, however late, to those who are still investigating the attacks of September 11.

One of Joe's superiors at Fresh Kills, FBI Special Agent Richard Marx, would later state that every day there was like September 12 for most of the workers. There was the eagerness to lend a hand, and the outpouring of energy and generosity. But there was also a closeness to destruction and death that kept stretching for months, even after Ground Zero had been swept clean. The Fresh Kills workers began to crave the experience of finding human remains. It's gruesome but precious, and undeniably strange, but meaningful nonetheless.

Joe recalls the workers' emotional response to finding remains:

"They were so happy 'cause they thought they'd done something good." Finding remains and thereby helping a family identify and honor a loved one fulfilled the purpose of their work. If the load they worked on wasn't "hot"—as they came to call a load with remains of the catastrophe, either human or industrial—Joe's team would often leave work dejected.

. . .

The morning of September 11, 2001, Joe was at his office at 300 Gold Street, right at the end of the Manhattan Bridge on the Brooklyn side, working on a report alongside the six detectives on his team.

"I don't even remember what the meeting was about now, but at that moment it was important," Joe says, underscoring how everything was about to change. He does remember that they were to present the report soon at One Police Plaza, the NYPD's headquarters in Lower Manhattan, near the World Trade Center.

Joe walked out of the room to make copies and came back shortly. "A plane just hit the World Trade Center," stated one of the female detectives. *Must have been a Piper Cub, or some other small plane,* Joe thought, not too worried, stroking his strong, square chin and smoothing out his signature white mustache. *Maybe the pilot had a heart attack.*

Someone else suggested they go up to the roof and take a look, since it was just a couple of flights up from their fifth-floor offices. The line of sight to the towers was perfectly clear, especially on that day, with its famously limpid sky. Joe's mild curiosity soon gave way to shock, as the group pointed and stared at the flames coming out of the North Tower.

Another detective came up with a portable radio. They learned the plane was an airliner. Still facing the Manhattan side, Joe felt someone forcefully grab his arm. It was his close friend and colleague, Lisa. The whole group turned their heads to the right to confirm the unthinkable: a second plane flying extremely low, starting to turn toward the other tower. The plane was so close that Joe could see the little oval outlines of the windows.

They all knew what was about to happen. The plane went across the Hudson River and crashed into the side of the building, its nose coming out the other side.

Joe felt like he could reach out and touch the flames. His eyes recorded the hit; his ears, the boom of the explosion; his skin, the whoosh of the heat. He looked at Lisa and said, "Oh my God. We're at war."

• • •

Joe was born in Brooklyn. He grew up, as he says, in a simpler time. His family life was stable. He spent much of his childhood hanging out with a group of ten or twelve neighborhood kids who all went to the local Catholic church. Their days were filled with school, and then, after school, playing ball outside. Joe and his gang traveled around the neighborhood to local ball games.

Police work was the Keenan family business. Joe's father was a policeman, his uncle was a policeman, and his cousin was a policeman. But Joe learned early on that you left business outside of the family home; his dad rarely discussed his work. His parents urged him to get an education and go into work that allowed for an easier, less dangerous life, but Joe was always drawn to the uniform and the idea of serving.

Joe met his wife, Jane, when they were both just fifteen years old. It was natural. Boys and girls were pairing up from the parish, and they were part of the same group. Jane and Joe were comfortable with each other and have remained so for the past forty-five years. Together they raised their three children, all of whom stayed nearby after leaving the nest. Life made sense to Joe and Jane, and family came first.

On September 11, Jane was the first person Joe called when he understood how serious the situation was. The assistant principal at the school where Jane worked in Park Slope answered, and Joe told her, "Just let Jane know I'm not *there*." He also advised that the students be kept at the school: "Don't let them out 'til we know what's happening." Joe promised to call back when it was safe to dismiss the students.

Joe's college-age son, Joseph, was on his way to class in Brooklyn. Karyn, the middle child, was at home preparing for a job interview later in the afternoon at, of all places, the World Trade Center. It was Janine, the eldest, who called him with a more frantic tone from her office on the west side of midtown.

"I can't find Andy!" said Janine, sobbing. She feared the worst had happened to her fiancé.

"You should stay where you are," Joe instructed.

But Janine was desperate to find Andy. "I'm leaving. I'm going down there," she said, then hung up the phone.

Joe knew Andy worked on Pine Street, a few blocks from the World Trade Center. There was nothing he could say to stop his headstrong daughter. Joe was worried, but he kept it to himself, not wanting to alarm the rest of the family.

Joe's whole detective squad, and all others in the building, went into rescue mode in a matter of minutes. They went down to the fifth floor to put on their uniforms and then gather into rank structure. They formed their own small army.

Before they left the building, they saw the first tower come down as they looked on through their office windows. The dust rose upward in a cloud, the loud crumbling sound lagging seconds behind. Joe slowly took in the magnitude of what had just happened. This was unlike anything they'd seen before.

• • •

The small army of police officers made their way across the Manhattan Bridge late that morning as orders began to trickle down from further up the ranks about where they could be of assistance. Crowds were streaming in the opposite direction, seeking refuge in Brooklyn. A man completely covered in dust, but still clutching his briefcase, sprinted past Joe. He was reminded of the pictures from Hiroshima and Vietnam as he saw the despair in people's ash-covered faces. Everyone was in shock.

As news about the attacks kept coming in, Joe discussed the best strategy for how to proceed with his team. They had limited information: The city was, indeed, in the midst of a terrorist attack, no one inside the planes could have survived, and officials feared that there might be another attack at street level. Beyond that, the police officers depended mostly on their instincts and drew on previous emergency experience, neither of which felt adequate in the face of such a huge disaster.

Joe's group was sent first to the Thirteenth Precinct in Manhattan and then to NYU Medical Center, which was expecting a large influx of injured civilians. But as Joe sadly and simply stated, "The wounded never came."

Hours passed at the NYU hospital. Joe, himself, was forced to receive treatment for irritation to his eyes, likely caused by all the chemicals floating around in the air after the attacks, as he waited for further instructions. He could only wonder, *What next?*, and fear made him assume the worst: riots, looting, terrorists on the ground gunning down more victims. As the day progressed, Joe kept a silent prayer going for his daughter Janine.

When Joe finally made it home well after midnight, his daughter Karyn and son, Joe, were together and still wide awake. "Janine and Andy are at Uncle Jerome's," Karyn said. "Janine ran into Andy on the street. She was running downtown, he'd been running uptown, and they found each other. Can you believe it?"

"A one-in-a-million chance" was all Joe could muster, his whole body relaxing with relief. It all sounded like a scene from a movie. Thankfully, this plot twist was an uplifting one.

Joe managed to salvage his last bit of energy to check his email before going to bed. His in-box was full of messages from police departments all over the country wanting to know what they could do. They were trying to figure out how to get to New York City as quickly as possible, even from cities as far west as San Francisco. As the city's police department kept stretching itself thinner and thinner to meet everybody's needs, the generosity of others was reassuring, and that spirit would stay with Joe for a long time to come.

· · ·

One of Joe's last assignments on the street, before his promotion to the Detective Bureau, was as a vehicular homicide detective. He had seen sights he never wished to see again: lives cut short, broken bodies young and old, scrap metal strewn on a highway from a crashed car. With decades under his belt, he thought he'd seen it all.

Then there was September 12 at Ground Zero. "We saw steel girders, maybe five feet around, completely twisted like pretzels from the heat," Joe recalls with a grimace. "Whoever was in there wasn't coming out."

In the coming months, Joe's assignment would be elsewhere, though he still traveled to Ground Zero at least once a day to gather or present information for the chief of detective offices.

He arrived at the Sixty-ninth Regiment Armory, on Lexington Avenue between Twenty-fifth and Twenty-sixth streets, to the sight of thousands of people lined up. He was charged with gathering information from families who had missing loved ones to report. "These poor people, they all had pictures," he says. "They all knew that their person was going to be okay. Husband, wife, mother, father, whatever it was. And we knew differently."

The Sixty-ninth Regiment building stands as the site of the only official Irish regiment in New York City, with a history that extends back to the Civil War. Under different circumstances, this impressive legacy might have emboldened Joe, proud as he has always been of his Irish roots, but the next two weeks under the main hall's imposing vaulted ceiling would forever haunt him.

Joe quickly felt the weight of this unprecedented task. The grizzly panorama at Ground Zero brought back painful images of his work investigating vehicular homicide. Working with the victims' families brought back a different but all-too-familiar emotion from those years: futility in the face of grief.

The Sixty-ninth Regiment building was once divided up into galleries full of electrifying paintings by Cézanne, Matisse, and Van Gogh in the early 1900s. It was now without decoration, sectioned into smaller squares by slim curtains. Detectives paired off and one by one interviewed throngs of sorrowful faces, questioning individuals inside the curtained spaces, asking them to describe their missing loved ones.

Joe went around the room, noticing the patterns of behavior in the victims as well as his own detectives. He was struck by the need to touch. "Invariably, one of the family members would hold the detective's hand as they were talking," Joe remembers, choking up. "And we talked with them for however long it took, knowing there was nothing we could do to help these poor people."

. . .

The armory was like a distressed beehive. Cops moved around the labyrinth of curtains gathering as much information as they could, often knowing their efforts would prove fruitless. The busyness was the only thing that might stave off the deep sadness, so people just kept moving.

Joe knew that the detectives themselves were crushed, some already suffering from secondary trauma, also known as compassion fatigue or vicarious traumatization by psychologists. He explains, "Some of the officers skipped meals and refused to take breaks. They were spending too much time with each subject and having a hard time controlling their emotions. They stayed late after they were finished and came early before their tour started. I was doing the same thing."

Recognizing that this behavior wasn't sustainable, Joe started insisting that people take care of themselves: "I made it a point to demand that they took breaks and ate meals. At that time I was not making friends, but in the years since, many detectives, even some I didn't know, have come to me and thanked me for being their 'boss' at that time."

Dr. Emanuel Shapiro, senior psychoanalyst and senior supervisor for therapists in training, spent many months in the fall of 2001 working with first responders and volunteers. He explains, "Secondary trauma is the therapist's or other crisis worker's symptomatic counterpart to the victim's post-traumatic stress disorder (PTSD). It is an occupational hazard of care providers, be they family, friends, therapists, medical professionals, or volunteers."

Caregivers are always at risk of becoming depleted and traumatized in their effort to take care of others. Trauma social worker and educator Laura van Dernoot Lipsky talks about the importance for first responders to practice the art of "trauma stewardship"—a daily practice of tending to the hardship, pain, or trauma of the world, while also being mindful about the kind of self-care necessary to make this practice sustainable.

"More than anything else, what we need in order to practice trauma stewardship is knowledge of our own lives—what we feel, value, and experience, and what we need to do to take care of ourselves," Lipsky writes. She recommends everything from meditation and a supportive community to creative outlets, such as playing music, dancing, and visual arts.

Sometimes the fatigue builds up simply from the experience of futility. Joe had been in this place many times before as a vehicular homicide detective: listening and nodding as a desperate family member shared his or her story, all the while thinking that there was no good news to give, that there would probably never be good news to share.

Just after Joe was informed that the victims' center was to be transferred farther uptown, he received a call from longtime friend

Deputy Inspector James Luongo. Luongo had been selected to be the NYPD's commanding officer for the recovery effort at Fresh Kills and was now in the process of recruiting his own handpicked team of trustworthy supervisors.

The time had come for Joe to do something difficult yet important for the families he'd been interviewing for the past two weeks. "I was completely drained by the experience at the victims' center," Joe remembers. "I just could not bear to be with people suffering and crying from broken hearts. It still affects me."

• • •

Because it is a Wednesday at Fresh Kills, Joe expects visitors. A few months after the site was established, the Office of the Mayor's Community Assistance Unit had started arranging for 9/11 victims' families to visit once a week in groups of twelve. Some of them bring flowers, hoping to pay their respects to loved ones. Without the comfort of a funeral or memorial service, complete with their loved ones' bodies, mourners are forced to make ad hoc rituals to find comfort and, possibly, a sense of closure at Fresh Kills.

Joe feels added pressure to prove that their work has been thorough and conducted with utmost respect, but his no-nonsense Irish American upbringing, as well as twenty-five years as a seasoned cop, tell him he shouldn't expect any praise. In fact, he expects the opposite. Police work is usually thankless. Joe knows that to the general public, the police are never "good news." They show up when there's crime, injury, and death. They bust down doors, ask intrusive questions, and take nothing for granted. They leave expensive fines, legal charges, and loss in their wake. Joe says that in order to be a good cop, "you need to understand where you stand in relation to people; you need to understand that as a cop, you're really dealing with people when they're having problems."

He's heard rumblings about families being upset with the work going on at Fresh Kills and the handling of the recovery more generally. Staten Island, long the butt of New Yorkers' jokes, is not known for being a pleasant haven, and here the city is, shipping the delicate remains to a former landfill on a daily basis. The recovery effort is slow, simply because it is so painstaking. This leaves some families waiting for their loved ones' remains, frustrated.

And yet, this Wednesday in early 2002, he's met with public recognition and appreciation, not frustration. A group of visitors bears a special gift for Joe and his team. The two groups run into each other around lunchtime, as Joe's team is about to take the bus up to the local mess hall, known to the workers as Hilltop Café. "We brought you cookies. Thank you for all the hard work you are doing for us," a young woman says as she hands over a tin box.

Joe and his team are stunned. The detectives don't eat their lunch at the mess hall, like usual. They share the cookies, relieved to have a sweet break from all the sadness of their eighteen-hour daily grind.

. . .

Once the summer of 2002 arrives, work is winding down at Fresh Kills. On an early July day, Joe wakes up at two thirty in the morning, his regular time, and tiptoes around the bed, careful not to wake Jane up.

As he drives from Brooklyn into Staten Island via the Verrazano Bridge, he remembers the first days at Fresh Kills. Before the debris of 9/11 crept in, it was a barren land of peaks, valleys, and creeks, just off the highway and yet disconnected from civilization. "The city on the hill," as they've come to call the site, was built of the trailers and laboratories, the cafeteria and rest center, the lampposts and roads, the sweat off their brows.

Fresh Kills served as a main New York City landfill for fifty years before it closed down in March of 2001. At one point in its history, it was also the world's largest. Residents of Staten Island were never thrilled by the dubious honor. If anything, it promoted the already discriminatory association of Staten Island with the city's dumping ground. That chapter had closed, and months later Fresh Kills began a new one: as the site of the city's largest crime scene ever.

Like archeologists digging into Pompeii's tragic past, their task was to recover as many personal effects and human remains as possible. Unlike the victims of that ancient volcano's eruption, the destruction here was man-made, at first requiring inspection for forensic evidence. To Joe's surprise, larger objects he would have assumed loomed among the debris were for the most part pulverized, not spared from destruction. They were more likely to find smaller objects, scraps of metal and bone fragments, rather than squashed desks or human limbs. The official tally would cite 4,257 pieces of human remains and fifty-four thousand personal effects recovered.

For Joe this had been an assignment like no other. For one, there was the unbelievable and sometime horrific scale of the task. Most important, it was the opportunity to bring hope to grieving families, something he often wished he could have done during all those years as a police officer in his neighborhood.

Joe also experienced his own dose of hope from other police departments around the country who made good on their promise of pitching in. After a massive fund-raising effort, members of the San Francisco Police Department got their wish to be present at Fresh Kills. Joe was also impressed with the officers from all over the East Coast who would drive to Staten Island during their own off-duty hours. They worked with Joe for two or three days before traveling back to their regular shifts. He would send them to Father Ryan, a Jesuit in charge of Staten Island's Mount Manresa retreat house, who was generous enough to host these off-duty cops and provide their meals. "It felt great to know that we had friends everywhere," Joe explains.

Joe was also proud to have given tours of Fresh Kills to President Bill Clinton and the royal chief medical examiner of Great Britain, who asked if Joe would be able to replicate a similar operation in England should anything, God forbid, similar happen there. Joe joked that he would have to ask his bosses, President Bush and Mayor Giuliani.

By seven thirty at night, Joe is already driving back home. Dinner with Jane awaits. Jane doesn't work summers, and Joe wonders what it will be like when they are both able to just up and leave, travel the world. Joseph and Karyn will probably be home too. Heading back to Brooklyn as the sun starts to set, Joe feels ready to move forward with his life. He can confidently describe his work at Fresh Kills as the "crowning jewel" in a career that he already loved. He says, "I'll never have to worry again about whether I did my job. That's important to guys like us. No matter what else I move on to, it'll never be as fulfilling as working here was."

. . .

Karyn, the middle child of the Keenan family, approached her father late one night in December of 2001, shortly after Joe had started working at Fresh Kills, and complained—as she had so many times before—about her unfulfilling job in the business sector. She reminded him that she had passed the Police Officer Entrance Examination years ago, but she was too young to join at the time. "I think I'm ready, Dad," she told him.

Joe had conflicting emotions about his daughter's decision: happiness and apprehension. On the one hand, he was proud to see how much his daughter craved meaningful work, and further, that she saw the same path he'd traveled for decades as one that truly mattered. On the other hand, he didn't want his baby girl in any danger. His advice was simple: "If you want to do it, you have to really want to do it."

By the time that Fresh Kills closed on July 31, 2002, Joe didn't want to "do it" anymore. He was sure that all of his co-workers felt the same: Everyone was glad about not having to come back tomorrow. He had not anticipated retiring so soon after finishing at Fresh Kills, but the long hours had piled up relentlessly, and Joe was exhausted and nursing a back injury. He officially retired on December 31, 2002, at the age of fifty-two.

There is something to be said about how the uniqueness of the task at Fresh Kills united the people in charge of it. Psychoanalyst Dr. Heinz Kohut talks about the concept of "twinship," which refers to the feeling of being drawn to other people whose circumstances and stories are similar to one's own. The workers at Fresh Kills were part of a select crew entrusted with a grueling and gruesome but special task. They worked side by side. Shoveling. Sifting. They stared into the rubble and recognized that vacant look of post-shock all too often. They got tired and complained. They held up with pride. They combed the debris together, shared moments of pride in finding any bit of remains. Most important, they shared an awareness; few people could know what it was like to be in their shoes.

The need for twinship, this feeling of a shared and special awareness, is lifelong—often emerging in intense experiences, like that of post-9/11 recovery. It allows us to remember, to normalize, to contain the trauma in a collective, soothing way. The men and women who worked at Fresh Kills, performing the same jobs, carrying the same tools, bonded by the same purpose, were, in a sense, twins for one another. Their shared commitment provided psychological support as they worked their way through the wreckage.

Joe and the other workers at Fresh Kills were bound not only to each other, but to the victims whose remains they were seeking. These victims had been dehumanized in the attacks, reduced to objects, to "things"—essentially no different from the towers themselves. The workers at Fresh Kills, sifting through the rubble for remains, sought to restore that humanity by providing the respect due to those victims, one small and reverent gesture at a time.

The question of what to do with the remains continues, all these years later. *The New York Times* reported:

In one of the haunting legacies of the terrorist attack on the World Trade Center, the remains of 1,123 of the victims, 41 percent of the total, have not been identified, leaving many of their relatives yearning for closure. At the same time, nearly 10 years later, 9,041 pieces of human remains— mainly bone fragments but also tissue that has been dehydrated for preservation—are still being sorted through by the city's medical examiner for DNA, though the last time a connection was made was in 2009.

The official plans for the September 11th Memorial and Museum include an effort to house all of the nearly 10,000 pieces of human remains still unidentified by the city seven stories below ground and behind a wall with a quotation from Virgil's *Aeneid* etched into it: "No day shall erase you from the memory of time." In this way, the institution honors its role as both museum—a place where meaning is made and history marked—and memorial, a place for actual mourning and sacred acknowledgement. The September 11th Memorial and Museum, after all, will literally be built on the hollowed ground where these lives were lost.

For some of the families who lost love ones, the idea of incorporating the remains into the institution in this way is troubling. They would prefer a separate memorial space, clearly delineated from the hustle and bustle that is sure to fill the museum on a regular basis. For others, it is the perfect medley of uses—learning and honoring, marking and mourning—for such a conflicted space. Only time will tell how this complex and deeply emotional and spiritual conversation evolves, but Joe is proud knowing that he did his best to make sure that as many families as possible had an opportunity for at least a modicum of closure.

• • •

Now that he's retired, Joe is involved in another kind of detective work: trying to figure out why his family doesn't know he is so funny. He's always thought of himself as a funny guy, ready to crack a joke at any moment. But his family seems to be in the dark about this personality trait, or at least it seems that way to Joe. They do laugh at the joke he tells about his retirement: "My last day of work was New Year's Eve, so the city threw me a big party."

His family might be wondering what is going on, but they are relieved to see a more relaxed version of Joe. For the first three months of 2003, his wife and children had to deal with a fidgety man not used to waking up late, not used to having no appointments or obligations.

His friends warned him that the worst time to retire from police work was winter, being forced to stay home with an extreme case of cabin fever, and they were right. While Joe's wife and children tended to work or studies during the day, he stayed home with the dog . . . reading, resting, and reflecting.

Joe says, "Now I do normal things. The unknown has been taken away. The edge you are prepared for is not there. I'm not as high with that. Now I'm going half-steam." And yet he knows Jane is happy that he's calmer and that she doesn't have to wait for him to come home. Now he waits for her to come home, and they worry together about their daughter Karyn, who graduated from the Police Academy and became a detective in the Organized Crime Control Bureau, Narcotics Division.

As for his sense of humor, Joe is starting to realize why his family is pleasantly surprised that he enjoys a good laugh. He explains, "When I was still working, I came home and kept thinking about cases that were going on. It might have made me more serious and grumpier than I wanted to be."

To this day, Joe regrets a rare outburst at Jane after he came back from a particularly gruesome day as a vehicular homicide detective. She could tell that something was troubling him and pushed for an answer. "What do you want me to tell you?" he responded to her. "Do you want me to tell you about the dead babies I saw today?" he shouted, his large, expressive eyes opened wide and accusatory at his shocked wife.

Now that Joe has gotten the hang of retirement, he offers, "It probably brings me more to the person I really am because I am relaxed, I can say what I want to say, do what I want to do, get involved with things that interest me."

• • •

It is an early afternoon in the spring of 2009, and Joe is leaving the house to go on one of his "little adventures." Janine and Andy's first child, Joe's granddaughter Alyssa, is now four years old and goes to preschool four blocks away. He is headed to pick her up.

Alyssa was born in May of 2005, an event that ranks among the most exciting in Joe's life. "To see your child have a child . . . it's a whole different feeling altogether than with your own children," Joe reflects. "I didn't think that, at this stage of life, we could enter another stage. It's amazing how a baby can change the activities of a whole family."

Janine drops Alyssa off in the morning at her grandparents' home; then Joe proceeds to walk her to school. He enjoys their conversations during these short walks and considers them quality time.

She's starting to become a little person, Joe thinks as he sees her walk out of her classroom, her small backpack strapped on tight.

The girl has Grandpa's big blue eyes. He grabs her tiny hand in his, and they walk down the steps, homeward bound.

The grandchildren are more than new lives to take care of; they've given Joe new life.

When Alyssa was born, the exhaustion from the recovery effort at Fresh Kills still loomed large in his mind and his body. On one particular day when Alyssa was just two months old, when Joe was visiting at Janine's house in nearby Valley Stream, he decided to take a walk to the park. Joe put the baby in her carriage and left the house. "Time started to slip," he remarks. His phone rang. It was his wife, Jane.

"Where are you?" she asked. Joe paused.

"You've been gone for two hours! Where are you?" she repeated.

"I'm just walking around town," he chortled. "I'll be right home."

Joe interprets the time slip as the baby becoming the new focus of his thoughts. When he talks about how Alyssa "cleared his head," it is as if she was finally clearing away the mess of Fresh Kills.

• • •

Joe's physical health, however, hasn't been so ideal. By 2005, he was sure he had the so-called World Trade Center cough that most first responders and workers were enduring. He went through periods of losing his voice as his infection worsened and had to contend with insomnia, a new experience for this hardened cop. Joe's doctors have operated on his sinuses and throat several times, even removing parts of his throat and tongue in order to reduce the swelling along his breathing passage.

Although Joe is a self-described coward for pain, he has been taking care of himself, keeping up with doctors' appointments year-round. He talks about it as "going in for fine-tuning." His nonchalance belies the wisdom he has gained: "Pain has a good effect on you. It slows you down a little."

During this past decade of Joe's life, he has slowed down a lot, sometimes by choice, sometimes not. The slower pace, the reduced intensity of his endeavors, the larger chunks of time he can dedicate to his family—all of these are pieces of his life found after the work at Fresh Kills was over, and perhaps because of it.

Budding poet Lauren Seaquist, the fourteen-year-old who won the Second Annual Fresh Kills Haiku Contest in 2010, writes: "Looking at the mounds / You are rolling down the past / Future brings us new."

Indeed. The World Trade Center recovery effort at Fresh Kills is the sad coda for the long-closed landfill. Still, just as the future held unexpected journeys for retired Sergeant Joseph J. Keenan, it also holds something new for this expanse of land almost three times as large as Central Park.

• • •

The seeds for Fresh Kills Park were sown weeks before 9/11, when the world's top architecture firms were scrambling to submit their proposals for developing the area into a large-scale urban park. After the attacks, the plans remained buried until 2003, when the competition was reopened.

On a Sunday morning in October of 2010, a crowd gathers at a parking lot behind a strip mall in Staten Island. There is enough of a chill in the air for the throng of visitors to put on their jackets as they line up. A tram transports the curious families, some with very young children in tow, into Fresh Kills Park for the general public's first sneak peek.

There is now a welcome center near Fresh Kills's heavily guarded entrance. Landscape architect Ellen Neises leads a "lecture" tour up the replanted northernmost mound, the second tallest on-site, standing 150 feet above sea level. As she walks up, she stops occasionally, pointing out the surrounding area while flipping through a large pamphlet of colorful plans. These plans were drawn up by her firm, James Corner Field Operations, which won the competition in 2003.

It is hard to tell how far the hilly landscape spreads north, away from the nearby highway and toward the faraway outline of Manhattan. It is even harder to imagine what the fully developed park will look like, with the proposed amphitheater, marina, and golf course. At the top of the hill that morning, children happily flew kites lifted high by the strong wind gusts that once slowed down the work of Joe and his detectives.

Fresh Kills has become a testament to a kind of fundamental truth—that we can't ever predict, as individuals or as a nation, what the future holds. Joe's life has changed so much. He reflects,

"I miss my friends from work—only another cop truly knows how to relate to another cop—but I am not aching to go back. I am content with the way things are now. It's simpler and much less stressful. Although things now are important in their own context, nothing really requires split-second life-changing decisions. Whatever comes, we deal with."

He goes on, "If I were twenty-five again, I would do it all over, but now someone else can do it. I'll remember the good times and try to live with the bad."

. . .

Paul Hawken, an environmentalist and entrepreneur, writes, "Birth and death are each other's consorts, inseparable and fast." Joe's story so clearly demonstrates this healing and universal pattern. Surrounded by death and destruction in its most gruesome form for months on end, Joe became intimate with the end of life and the worst of humanity's destructive impulses. As difficult as this experience was, it opened him up in a way that allowed him to truly appreciate his granddaughter's birth, and two new grandsons after that: Michael, born in October of 2008, and Joseph Jerome IV, born in August of 2010.

It is not uncommon for families that have just lost someone dear to learn that one of their own is pregnant. The cycle of life seems at its most insistent following death's unexpected arrival; it's as if birth is just waiting in the wings, ready to fill the broken open hearts of those in mourning.

Advancing Is Perfection

Debbie Almontaser

D ebbie Almontaser was disappointed on her very first morning in America.

"I went to the window, looked outside, and there was this huge blanket of white everywhere," she remembers. Debbie, a curious three years old at the time, had just emigrated from Yemen. She ran all around the house and shouted out to the rest of her family: "You have to wake up! There's sugar everywhere! We have to get the buckets! We have to get the pans!"

Her parents giggled and explained, "Honey, it's not sugar."

"What do you mean?" she asked.

"It's not sugar. It's snow."

Her indignant retort: "No, this is America! This is where everybody comes. This is where you have everything you want."

Her father then led young Debbie to the window, opened it, and let her touch the snow. The child was not so easily discouraged. She asked her father if she could taste it, thinking it might just be cold sugar.

"To my disappointment," she recalls, "it tasted like nothing."

• • •

Debbie's imagination, rooted in those early years, never really waned. It was part of what made her a fantastic teacher. One day, while giving a lesson to her fifth graders at P.S. 261 in downtown Brooklyn, she heard a knock on the classroom door.

"Can I speak to you in the hallway?" asked a PTA representative, poking her head in.

Debbie turned to her eager students and handed a marker to one of the boys, telling him, "Why don't you finish the math problem with the rest of the group? I'll be back in just a moment."

She stepped outside and was immediately struck by how grave the expression on the parent's face was: "We have just found out that one of the World Trade Center towers has been hit by a plane. We don't know how it happened, but we're speculating it was an accident."

Debbie's heart dropped into her stomach. The image of a plane crashing into a skyscraper played across her mind. The parent informed her that the administration was requesting that all children be kept in the classroom until further notice. "Don't alarm them," she added. "You can do it."

Left in the hallway alone, Debbie took a deep breath and then headed back into her classroom.

. . .

Debbie left Yemen at the tender age of three, along with her mother, to reunite with her father, who had previously left for the United States. He had gone in search of a job and had found one, as a steelworker at the Ford Motor Company in Buffalo, New York.

Debbie's only recollection of Yemen is her departure from it. "I remember the steps of the plane being very high, and in between them there was this hollow space, and it was really windy," she describes. "And I remember my mother holding my hand and dragging me up." Debbie was afraid that the wind would blow her tiny body right through the hollow spaces in between the steps.

As an immigrant child in Buffalo during the seventies, she struggled to fit in. While the other girls wore name-brand outfits and played with the latest and most expensive toys, Debbie was usually dressed in one of her mother's creations, with her nose in a book. Her parents encouraged her not to stand out as different among her classmates, and yet they sent her to Sunday school to learn Arabic language and culture. She knew that simply by virtue of being Arab, she automatically didn't fit in, and in some ways, it compelled her to stand out even more deliberately.

"One day in seventh grade, I decided to wear the *hijab*," Debbie remembers. "I went to school and everyone was looking at me so strangely."

Upon spotting her in her headscarf, her girlfriends shouted, "You look silly! That's not you! Take it off!"

"Why are you wearing that?" asked one of her usually supportive teachers. "Did you know that women are oppressed by wearing that? You wearing it shows you're inferior."

"Inferior"—the word reverberated inside of Debbie, causing confusion and shame. In her Islamic cultural class, she'd learned that wearing the *hijab* was simply a way of signifying modesty and a desire for privacy for Muslim women—something that Debbie often craved in the chaotic atmosphere of her junior high school. And here her teacher was shaming her into feeling as if she'd done something terribly wrong. It took at least a decade for Debbie, then living in New York City with her husband, to embrace the garb of her tradition with renewed confidence. Still, the sting of her teacher's humiliation would stay with her for a lifetime.

• • •

Debbie, called "Miss A" by her students, closed the door and went back into her classroom, to the tall bookshelf she had there. She picked out one of her favorite books, *The Hundred Dresses,* by Eleanor Estes. In it, Wanda Petronski, a poor Polish immigrant girl, is ridiculed by her classmates because of her funny name, imperfect accent, and limited wardrobe.

"Today we're going to do things a little bit differently, class.

Instead of reading independently, I'm going to read this story aloud to you," Debbie told the squirming bunch before her. "It's one of my favorites."

"Mine too!" shouted a student in the back.

"Well, good, let's get started," Debbie said, smiling to hide the anxiety starting to build up in her body. She held the book open and out to the side so the students could get a good look at the beautiful illustrations as the story unfolded. *"Today, Monday, Wanda Petronski was not in her seat. But nobody, not even Peggy and Madeline, the girls who started all the fun, noticed her absence."*

Debbie read these words, but all the while there was a second story unfolding in her increasingly anxious mind. She wondered who was responsible for the plane flying into the tower. Was it an accident? A recreational pilot somehow way off course? *"Wanda did not sit there because she was rough and noisy. On the contrary she was very quiet and rarely said anything at all."*

Debbie tried to recall all of the recent terrorist attacks. The suicide bombing of the USS *Cole* in October of 2000 in Yemen came to mind. Could this be one as well? It was awful to even entertain the thought. She wondered if any of her students' parents worked in the towers. *"Then sometimes they waited for Wanda—to have fun with her."*

There was a second knock on the door. It was the same parent. Debbie set the book down gently and assured her students that she'd be right back, then headed out into the hallway again. "The second tower was hit. We no longer think it was an accident."

Debbie shuddered.

"Debbie, don't lose it!" said the parent. "You are fortunate that you can't see anything from your windows. In the classrooms facing the skyline, the kids are by the windows, and some of the teachers are in a state of shock. You have to be strong for your kids."

As she walked back inside, Debbie spotted smoke trailing far across the sky outside the hallway's windows. She picked up the book again and said, "Now, where were we?" hoping the students didn't notice that her arm was shaking as she held up the book. "Ah, I see. Here we were," she said, and began reading again. *"The next day, Tuesday, Wanda was not in school either."*

• • •

Just steps away from P.S. 261 lies the stretch of Atlantic Avenue known to the local Arab community as "Little Syria." Tourist buses stop by every day to let their passengers buy baked goods, spices, and other treats at favorite vendors. The finger-pointing and scape-goating had taken hold just hours after the attacks.

As the children continued to get picked up through the early afternoon, one Arab American mother approached Debbie in hysterics. "What happened?" asked Debbie, trying to calm her down and find a quiet place to talk away from the other parents.

"As I was walking toward the building, a tall man came out from a group of parents standing there and said to me, 'It's you and your people who've done this to us! You bastards!'"

"People are angry right now," Debbie told the woman, giving her a hug. "They don't know how to deal with it." Debbie wished she could do more to comfort the aggrieved woman. She hated to see the ways in which the attacks were already breeding misunderstandings between people who were otherwise neighbors, dependent on one another to keep their communities and schools vibrant.

Once all the children had been picked up by their parents or caregivers that day, Debbie was finally able to head home to West Midwood, Brooklyn, and tend to her own family. She hugged her two younger children—Shifa and Mohammed—extra long, with great relief, and then asked, "Where is Yousif?" Her eldest son was often the one she worried about most.

Naji, her husband, said sadly, "Well, he was here, but he's already left . . ."

He went on to explain that Yousif, just eighteen years old, had already been deployed to the World Trade Center site in order to aid in the rescue mission. Upon his high school graduation, Yousif had convinced Naji and Debbie to sign papers permitting him to join the National Guard. Debbie hadn't felt good about it at all but knew that keeping her stubborn son from something, once he'd set his mind on it, wasn't a winning proposition.

Sitting at the dining room table that night after the attacks and staring at Yousif's empty seat was unbearable for Debbie. She couldn't eat. She couldn't calm down. She was flooded with guilt— why had she signed that stupid form? All she could think about was her sweet son, who right at that very moment was witnessing unspeakable carnage.

Her husband pointed out that her anxiety was upsetting for their other two children, and she tried valiantly, but not very successfully, to manage her fear. But soon, she would have welcome distraction from her son's absence.

The following day she received a call from the president of the school board to request her attendance at a meeting. "We need your input in this whole situation," he said, citing her history of leadership within the New York educational community on issues of diversity and justice.

There was silence as Debbie processed what was being requested of her, and then the superintendent's voice chimed in: "Debbie, I need you to come in tomorrow, whether school is open or not . . . You need to help us figure out what we can do."

Like her son who had been so suddenly called to action, Debbie was willing and able to pitch in.

• • •

New York City educators were among the unsung heroes on September 11, 2001. Linda Lantieri, the director of the Inner Resilience Program, an organization that provided retreat experiences and ongoing support for teachers affected by the terrorist attacks and their aftermath, attests: "Miraculously, due to quick thinking, deep caring, and the inner resourcefulness of educators in the area, not a single student life was lost."

After 9/11, countless educators were transformed overnight into grief counselors, recovery coordinators, and crisis-intervention experts for their students. As Lantieri visited schools in the aftermath of the attacks, she saw educators struggling to cope: "Many displayed the classic signs of compassion fatigue. In all the listening, they had not yet had the chance to check in with their own feelings and tell their own stories."

Such was certainly the case for Debbie. Although she was experiencing her own season of trauma, she rarely spoke about it to others—instead focusing on her students, her community work, anything to make her feel a sense of purpose in such an uncertain time. Mary Dluhy, director of group initiatives at Georgetown University and a therapist in private practice in Washington, D.C., explains, "When you are processing a loss—whether of a loved one or for a dream shattered—your deepest fears of abandonment, of helplessness, and of loss of control are triggered."

• • •

Being able to channel one's trauma and anxiety into a compelling project, as Debbie did, can be very healing. But nothing could prevent her from worrying about her son. Yousif would call home to let his family know he was all right, but he offered few details of his duties other than that he had been helping to recover bodies and to patrol the area.

"It is a world without time," he explained to his mother. "We don't sleep here. You eat when you get hungry." She could do nothing to protect him from the sights and sounds he was being exposed to. Though she had never witnessed such death and destruction firsthand, she could only imagine the way it must be embedding itself into her dear Yousif's mind. She felt as if she could do nothing to protect him.

On October 6, 2001—twenty-five days after the initial attack—Yousif got his first opportunity to come home from Ground Zero. When Debbie opened the door at about eight p.m. that autumn evening, Yousif was just standing there. "I couldn't believe it was him," she recalls. "It didn't look like him. His face looked so tired and so stressed; his clothes smelled. It was just so scary to look at him."

He broke the silence: "I am hungry."

The family sat together in a daze, watching Yousif eat. If Debbie had felt guilty before about allowing such a young person to join the army, now she felt sure that Yousif's experiences at Ground Zero had aged him. "How is it out there?" she asked tentatively.

Yousif took a few more forkfuls of the food on his plate, as ravenous as if he hadn't eaten once in the almost four weeks he'd been gone, and then said, "Mom, I can't begin to tell you. I would never, ever want you or Dad to see anything I saw. Mom, it's like going to hell and coming back."

. . .

Debbie was spending her school days inside the comforting bubble of her little classroom, but working with the school district on what was equivalent to a second job after hours. She explains, "My new-found activism was a way to help me deal with my issues around my son not being home and being at Ground Zero in a dangerous situation."

Her own mission was clear: promoting religious understanding during this volatile time. This included making sure that no one in the local school communities felt marginalized. She supervised the translation of school board communications with parents into as many languages as possible, did sensitivity training for fellow teachers, and gave talks to parents. She was also the first one that parents knew they could go to if their families experienced harassment or discrimination in or around school.

One of Debbie's favorite projects involved organizing groups of diverse students to discuss their experiences of September 11, 2001, and then paint murals together. Participating children were asked to reflect on questions like these in small groups: Where were you on 9/11? How did you feel when you heard about 9/11? What are your thoughts today about 9/11? What are your thoughts about the upcoming anniversary of 9/11?

She'd seen many children break into tears, expressing their sadness and fear—sometimes for the first time—over what happened that day. "One of the children who cried," Debbie recounts, "talked about the fact that his name was Osama Muhammed, and how his life was never going to be the same again. People will know he's Muslim and will torment him."

Debbie felt that the attacks had fanned the flames of ignorance, like that which she'd encountered as a little girl in Buffalo. It now had a grown-up name, Islamophobia, and it was becoming more and more rampant in the post-9/11 world.

According to the *Journal of Applied Social Psychology*, People of Middle Eastern descent experienced 354 attacks in 2000 and an astonishing 1,501 attacks in 2001. Among those who were victims of the backlash, a Middle Eastern man in Houston, Texas, was shot and wounded by someone accusing him of "blowing up the country," and four immigrants were shot and killed by a man who claimed to be taking revenge against Arabs (although only one of the victims, in reality, was of Arab descent) for the September 11th attacks.

In the face of this kind of violence, Debbie believed, educating the public about diversity and religious pluralism was more critical than ever. It had also become even more important for Muslims and Arabs to have a strong, peaceful voice in public.

. . .

In the summer of 2005, Debbie was at a gala breakfast banquet at Gracie Mansion, the historic residence where the Office of the Mayor holds significant events. Thanks to the instrumental work of Debbie and others, Mayor Michael Bloomberg had declared the week of July 9 to 16 the first-ever Arab American Heritage Week.

Debbie had served as the liaison between the mayor's office and the dozens of diverse Arab American organizations involved in the day's celebration. Between safety concerns and everyone wanting to make sure their interests were represented and their work recognized, hers was no easy task.

But Debbie was used to controversy. That past summer, she had intervened when the committee for the United American Muslim Day Parade printed flyers with the year's theme: "The Koran: Salvation of Humankind."

"I looked at it, and it just made me cringe," Debbie recalls. She went to her husband, who initially didn't see anything wrong with the flyer. She asked him, "What if you are a human being that does not believe in the Koran? What if your book is the Torah or the New Testament?"

"It didn't even dawn on me," Naji replied, but proudly threw his support, once again, behind his conscientious wife. Debbie presented her concern at a committee meeting, invited dialogue, and asked them to generate some new ideas.

"Well, do you have a title for us?" asked one of the committee members. She had come ready with a friend's suggestion for rewording the theme: "The Koran: A Universal Message."

It was her constant attention to the importance of language and her commitment to speaking in universal terms that made Debbie such a successful translator between the diverse Arab and Muslim American communities that she loved and the world of New York City politics. Debbie cried as the commissioner of immigration affairs, himself from the Dominican Republic, acknowledged Arabs' contributions to the city since the 1800s. She saw the beauty of receiving recognition from someone of another underrecognized culture.

When the mayor took the stage in July of 2005 and said, "Ahlan wa Sahlan. Welcome," Debbie smiled at the sound of Arabic and English intertwined in power's mouth.

. . .

Meanwhile, things had been continuously difficult for Yousif. Since the end of his service at Ground Zero in February of 2002, he had been plagued by nightmares. It was also hard for him to commit to anything: Jobs came and went, he started college but then dropped out, and stable relationships eluded him. Debbie had tried to convince him to go to therapy, but he had declined.

Yousif had to go see a doctor when his hair started falling out in patches. He also suffered from skin discoloration around his lips, which made him extremely self-conscious. The doctor suggested that these temporary symptoms were probably stress related. Debbie couldn't help thinking that these physical conditions were a result of the months he'd spent at Ground Zero, but she was even more concerned about her son's mental well-being.

Debbie cringed when she remembered the moment in January of 2003 when two detectives had shown up at her home, unannounced, and told her two boys—in her absence—that they had a few questions. The detectives were especially interested in information regarding anti-American comments their mother had supposedly made. Mohammed tried his best to defend his mother: "We're not that kind of family. My mom would never say anything anti-American. You don't know my mom."

In a conference call later that evening, one of the detectives explained, "Ma'am, we received an anonymous tip from a woman who had overheard you bragging about a son who went to train in Yemen and is now a National Reservist in the [U.S.] army."

Debbie kept her cool but didn't hide her indignation. After all, Yousif had not only admitted to them that he had visited his mother's native Yemen in the summer, but he had also identified himself as a proud American who had served in the rescue at Ground Zero.

She responded to the investigators, "We are Yemeni Americans, sir, and my son loves this country, the country he was born and raised in, and wants to serve."

At first, Yousif had been in support of the Iraq War, feeling that it was the necessary retaliation for the horrible carnage that he witnessed at Ground Zero. But when he sat, hip to hip, with his parents and watched the bombs being dropped on Baghdad, the reality of the violence set in. He came to see that America was creating more destruction, more Ground Zeros for other people's young sons to sort through. He didn't want anyone to see the things that he had seen.

He began educating himself more and more about the terrorist attacks, Al-Qaeda, the Bush administration, and all of the other complex facets of the moment that Americans were facing. Yousif's newfound knowledge made it difficult for him to continue his military commitment, but he ultimately decided to see his time commitment through and be discharged honorably. In the meantime, the reality that he could be deployed to Iraq at any time was paramount in his mind—perhaps part of why he had yet to plant his feet firmly on the ground.

. . .

Though Debbie continued to worry about Yousif, even larger opportunities to spread her message of religious pluralism were coming her way. In April of 2005, New Visions for Public Schools, a leading nonprofit in the education reform movement, contacted her to inform her that she had been recommended as the perfect person to head a dual-language Arabic and English school. It would be the first public school of its kind in the nation. "This will be your opportunity to bridge East and West," the leadership at New Visions told Debbie.

At first, she was a bit skeptical. There was still so much violence, discrimination, and harassment going on toward Middle Easterners in New York and beyond. Getting Arab American Heritage Week had been a feat in and of itself; there was still a lot of opposition to anything that uninformed people associated with the culture of terrorism. Was it really possible to get such a school off the ground and running?

But for all of her skepticism, Debbie had too much excitement about the possibility not to dedicate herself—heart and soul—to this new project. She saw the school as the potential culmination of everything she had worked for in her career and a beautiful expression of her most deeply held values about the importance of education in pursuit of a more peaceful world.

She spent the next two years taking the school from a dream on paper to a bricks-and-mortar reality—a place destined to be filled with bright students, well-trained teachers, and a diversity of learning opportunities. "I've surrounded myself with amazing people who believe in what the school stands for," she shared excitedly in 2006.

Everything was designed around one central question, the one that Debbie believed could serve as an inoculation against any ignorance that the children might be exposed to: How can I see myself in others?

In her excitement over the upcoming opening of the school, the Kahlil Gibran International Academy, Debbie quoted anthropologist Margaret Mead: "Never doubt that a small group of thoughtful, committed citizens can change the world. Indeed, it is the only thing that ever has."

But, as Debbie was to learn, a small group could also commit to bring down those efforts.

. . .

As far as Debbie knows, the rumors started online the summer before the school was to open. Several bloggers, who categorically opposed the opening of a school that included curriculum on Arabic language and culture, began investigating Debbie's past, determined to smear her and take down the school.

As numerous untrue rumors circulated, Debbie was too busy actually building the school community to pay too much attention. Her request for a public relations director was never fulfilled, so she decided to keep her head down and hope the storms would pass. She had a school to create.

Then came the blow that brought it all crashing down.

The phrase "Intifada NYC" had been printed on a T-shirt sold at a summer festival in Brooklyn's Prospect Park. The offices of the organization selling the T-shirt were located on the same floor as SABA, a Yemeni American association that Debbie had founded along with three neighbors. Ironically, SABA had just won a prestigious Union Square Award in 2006, for which they had been nominated anonymously, to boot, for their grassroots activism and work at building community.

The tenuous connection between Debbie and the T-shirts was exploited in the media to raise public suspicion of her as someone who would use her position as principal of the Arabic-English, dual-language school to proselytize to students, or even worse, promote a violent uprising.

As far as Debbie understands, some of her superiors were at a loss as to how to handle the situation, while others were blindly optimistic that the controversy would die down. The facts showed that the T-shirts had nothing to do with her, and even less with the school, which is why she was strongly encouraged by the Department of Education to give an interview, though her gut told her otherwise.

Debbie recalls how the interviewer asked her what the root meaning of the word "intifada" was, to which she gave a neutral response. She explained that its etymological origin is "shaking off," although it has taken on more violent connotations recently.

Her full answer, however, did not make it to print. The title of the article was "City Principal is 'Revolting,'" giving the public a fearmongering message: It is a danger to the city to have such an out-of-touch principal, who defended such inflammatory T-shirts, educating our children.

Never mind that T-shirts and the sayings printed on them are considered free speech. Never mind that Debbie had nothing to do with the shirts. Never mind that the actual answer she had given the interviewer was a thorough, informed definition of the word. She had failed to condemn "Intifada NYC," as the public wanted her to, and so she would lose the opportunity to lead the school of her dreams, blood, sweat, and tears. Debbie was forced to resign.

. . .

Debbie mourned her school as one might mourn a lost child. It was hard to believe that something that she had worked that hard on could be taken from her so easily. Her only consolation was that the Kahlil Gibran International Academy would go on without her. It would be an institution that would outlast the petty controversies and vitriolic bloggers. It would educate children in the beauty of diverse cultures and, ironically, the value of really hearing and learning from those unlike oneself.

The school did open on September 4, 2007, under a new principal, with only a sixth grade to pilot the school. The Kahlil Gibran International Academy has since relocated to downtown Brooklyn, near the Navy Yard, sharing a space with P.S. 287 and housing 108 students from grades six to eight.

Kahlil Gibran himself, as if anticipating Debbie's difficult journey, wrote hundreds of years ago, "Advance, and never halt, for advancing is perfection. Advance and do not fear the thorns in the path, for they draw only corrupt blood."

Debbie would continue to advance. In March of 2010, the U.S. Equal Employment Opportunity Commission ruled that she had been pushed out of her leadership position in a discriminatory manner. "It was the most incredible vindication anyone could ask for," Debbie says. She was glad that the story made print in major media like the New York Times. Although this turn of events lent Debbie's argument the needed weight should she decide to sue her employer, she decided not to. She didn't want to endure the emotional toll that a lengthy lawsuit would entail. "I couldn't imagine dealing with another six years of litigation," she explained. "For what? For money? That was not my intention from the beginning."

In fact, Debbie is still employed by the Department of Education. She now works as the special education department coordinator at a school in another part of Brooklyn, the Benjamin Banneker Academy, where she has had the opportunity to expand her own horizons and work with a largely African American population, a significant percentage of whom are Muslim.

Debbie would rather focus on the future than the past. She is now pursuing a Ph.D. in urban leadership education at Fordham

University. Her expectation is to develop a certification program for teachers of Arabic language and culture so that more schools like Kahlil Gibran can flourish under the aegis of the best minds within the upcoming generation.

. . .

To Debbie's great relief, Yousif honored his full commitment to the military without being deployed to war. Civilian life has been a struggle for him, but he is making his way. An engaging stint as an expediter—a liaison between the New York City Department of Buildings and local architects—set him in the right direction. He developed communication and negotiation skills, like his mother, that would help him later secure a job in the hotel industry, like his father. "He is throwing himself into his work—really trying to find himself," Debbie explains.

One day, as Debbie was walking with Yousif along Battery Park City, near Ground Zero, her son started recounting what it was like down there when he was serving with the National Guard. He described the blanket of dust that covered everything and the buckets they had used to clear it all out. He talked about the other guys, the dark moments, the tender volunteers.

"Maybe you should tell your story," Debbie suggested, enthralled but also concerned about her child, whom she sensed had been bottling up so many horrific memories. He nodded quietly. For now, she would have to be heartened by these small moments of openness between the two of them, and the hope that one day, he would tell her all that he had experienced and unburden himself once and for all.

. . .

There was so much lost, but still so much to be grateful for. This ties into one of Debbie's favorite Muslim traditions. She explains, "I love it when Ramadan falls during the same time as Thanksgiving, because I feel then that the whole country is observing in this time of thankfulness and reflection."

Debbie explains that the intention of fasting throughout the month of Ramadan is to reconnect with those who are less fortunate, a time for one to feel the hunger pains, and a time to reconnect with everything that God has given us that is sacred.

On the last day of Ramadan in 2009, Yousif found a beautiful reason to be grateful. He was on the subway platform in Brooklyn, munching on a beef patty as he waited for the Q train to Manhattan, when he saw a young woman standing nearby that he simply could not take his eyes off of. When the train slid into the station they both stepped onto the same car and struck up a conversation.

"Are you Muslim?" she asked boldly.

"Yes, why?" Yousif responded.

"Do you know it's Ramadan and you are eating a beef patty?" she asked, smiling playfully at having "caught him," before exiting the train.

"Wait!" Yousif bolted from his seat, although he had a few more stops to go, and jumped onto the platform beside her. "Can I call you sometime?"

Yousif and Bedor (a name that means "the sky before the sunrise") got married on Valentine's Day of 2010.

. . .

Grieving is most directly associated with the death of a loved one, but human beings are—in truth—exposed to so many different kinds of losses in one lifetime. We lose our faith. We lose our way. We lose our innocence. We must mourn the passing of time and weather the constant changes that besiege our lives—sometimes welcomed, sometimes resisted with all our futile might. Just as we process the death of a loved one in fits and starts, rather than linearly, just as we can't predict which moments will be most difficult and which will actually prove endurable—losing one kind of life and inheriting another can be a daunting experience.

For Debbie, September 11, 2001, marked the moment when her struggles and her purpose became simultaneously amplified. Before that Tuesday, she was a Muslim woman, aware of what it was like to be misunderstood, committed to fostering dialogue, but blessed with the luxury of pursuing pluralism with a quiet, deliberate commitment. After that Tuesday, she was plucked from her classroom, elevated and illuminated, burdened with tremendous responsibility, defamed and defrauded, and, ultimately, vindicated.

Today, she heals. She mourns a time when it was just her and the kids in the classroom, before the towers fell, before Islam became a

Rorschach test for fear and ignorance. She can't unhear the stories of hatred and violence that she has heard from her Muslim sisters and brothers, but what she *can* do is carry on their courage and grow even more impassioned to fight ignorance at the root. She has experienced, firsthand, the ways in which fear, unexamined, rots and turns into indiscriminate anger and blind hatred.

Debbie was not given her school, but she was given her son, and for this she is very grateful. Meanwhile, she will continue to fight for the nation that she believes is possible—one where children don't grow up disappointed in the country they have inherited, but instead have a chance to "advance, and never halt, for advancing is perfection."

Becoming Whole Again

Tanya Villanueva Tepper

At sunset, Tanya rides her motorcycle, "Big Daddy," over a Miami highway at top speed. The wind blows past her face, her hair shooting out behind her. She looks out at the horizon—sea, sky, and art deco architecture—and her heart and mind are lulled by the lush landscape and the loud sound of her machine. Her sadness and anger, her painful memories and fears about the future, are drowned out by the simple pleasure of riding, fast and free. There is nothing but the elements, this moment, the movement of letting go.

Tanya, at just thirty-five years old, has been forced to do an unusual amount of loving and letting go. She has had to be impossibly strong in the face of senseless loss. She has had to mourn.

Repeatedly. She has had to sit still and feel what no one ever wants to feel.

But when she climbs onto the bike, the whole world rushes by, her eyes give up fighting to focus on any one thing, and it all becomes a soothing blur. There is nothing to hold on to, so there is nothing to lose.

. . .

Tanya was not always a biker chick. In Queens, New York, in the fall of 2001, you would be more likely to find her flipping through candle or home-furnishing catalogs in her store, Inner Peace, or pasting pictures of gowns into her wedding-planning album. She was thirty-three. She was madly in love with her Argentinean fire-fighter fiancé, Sergio, and she was planning, planning, planning.

On the evening of September 10, 2001, Sergio called from the firehouse to tell her good night. They chatted about a few things—the store, the next day's election, their plans to book the wedding hall on Thursday—while Tanya played solitaire on the computer. Since they'd become engaged, Sergio and Tanya loved to talk about the future—the twin babies they hoped to have, where they were going to live, what kind of vacations they would take. Their future together felt truly blessed.

When they hung up, Tanya was struck by the realization that she'd been distracted. She hadn't given her man her full attention. She wondered if he'd noticed. Probably not. Sergio was characteristically happy-go-lucky. He knew that Tanya was entirely devoted to him, that she loved him with every ounce of her being. But just in case, she shot off a quick email to him with three simple words: "I love you." She fell asleep content.

She was painting her nails and watching the news the next morning when it was announced that a plane had flown into the World Trade Center. Tanya started calling everyone. "Did you hear?" she asked her mom. "Did you hear?" she asked Sergio's mom, with whom she was very close. The thought that Sergio might be there, that he might be in danger, hadn't crossed her mind. It was shocking but not yet personal.

But little by little, the realization that Sergio very well might be down there amid the smoke and confusion started to creep into her consciousness. Of course he would go; he would want to help his friends. She called the firehouse, Ladder 132 in Prospect Heights, Brooklyn, a couple of times, but she got a busy signal. Her fear grew, incrementally, perilously. Her senses suddenly felt superhero sharp. She watched. She listened. She waited, nails half painted.

And then the first tower collapsed. Tanya let out a primal scream. A thought flashed across her mind: *Sergio's in there,* but it was followed by an indignant, *No, he's not.* She began talking herself down, "He's on his way home. Call his cell. He's on his way home." She called his cell and got his voice mail.

Within the hour, people started showing up at her apartment. By noon, thirty people filled her living room. The vigil for Sergio began.

• • •

Tanya had let out a scream that primal only once before. It was the day she learned the true story of her mother.

Tanya was born in the Netherlands in June 1968 to a German mother, Sigrid, and a Filipino father, who was at that time engaged to someone else in his home country. A few months after Sigrid gave birth to Tanya, she left the baby with family and a promise that she would send for the baby once she'd found work and started a new life. Sigrid was overwhelmed and desperate—trying to make ends meet, strapped with debt, and in a tumultuous relationship. On December 17, 1968, a few days before Sigrid was supposed to arrive home for the Christmas holidays, she killed herself.

Tanya knew she was adopted at the age of twelve—by her father's brother Emilio, and his wife, Eileen, whom she was with since birth, but she never understood what happened to her mother until she traveled to Germany when she was twenty-seven. Her uncle on her maternal side unveiled the truth.

Sergio was the one who gave Tanya the final push and the emotional support that she needed to make the daunting trip. She had such a happy childhood, such a wonderful family, that she had wondered about the wisdom of seeking out what could only be a sad story. And yet, she could never quite shut off her curiosity. Even as a little girl—growing up in the Netherlands until she was two, then in London until she was six, and on to New York—she'd always felt different from her siblings. When she was eight years old, she asked her parents if she was adopted for the first time. She'd met her biological father, even met her half siblings, but she'd never known the truth about her mother.

Sergio came with her to Germany and held her hand as she learned the cruel news that her mother had been in pain so insurmountable that she'd ended her own life, even though her own daughter's was just beginning. At the hotel later that night, Tanya traced the letters *I-L-O-V-E-Y-O-U* on Sergio's back. She felt such a sense of relief. She'd faced the thing she was most afraid of with the man she loved.

. . .

Sergio and Tanya's first kiss was on June 30, 1994, in Miami, Florida—where Tanya was living at the time and Sergio had just come for a visit. He had a healthy head of black hair and thick, dark eyebrows, and he wore a white V-neck T-shirt that would end up see-through by the end of their sweaty night of dancing together. He was a playboy, to be sure, but Tanya sensed something deeper underneath all of his bravado.

They spent five straight days together—making love, laughing, and talking about growing up in the same neighborhood in Queens and their shared taste in music. When Sergio brought up the book *Many Lives, Many Masters*—the story of a skeptical psychiatrist's experience with channeling and reincarnation—Tanya's suspicion was confirmed. She thought, "Wow, not only is he this supermacho man, but he has this spiritual side to him."

He returned to New York and their whirlwind romance slowed down a bit. Tanya tried to play it cool but was determined not to let

Sergio forget her. She sent him funny cards, called him every once in a while, wished him a happy birthday when July Fourth rolled around. As subtle as she tried to be, there was no denying it. Nobody made her feel the way Sergio did. In 1995, she moved back to New York to, as they say, see about a boy.

• • •

By two a.m. on Wednesday, September 12, 2001, Tanya learned that Sergio was officially on the missing list. By Wednesday afternoon, Sergio's name suddenly disappeared from the missing list. Everyone let out wild cheers and started crying with relief, but there was still no information about where he was or what had happened to him. The euphoria wouldn't last long. On Thursday, September 13, 2001, Sergio's name mysteriously reappeared on the horrible list.

Tanya then got busy making a missing poster, as she'd learned other family members were doing. Only the best for her Sergio. She made about thirty color copies and passed them out to friends, giving the marching orders—*Put them up everywhere and anywhere. We must find Sergio and bring him home. He's out there.*

By Thursday, the majority of her initial visitors had gone home. Tanya realized that she'd need to keep people posted, so she started to send out emails. The first one read:

I really appreciate all of the support and prayers and Sergio will be amazed at all the people who rallied to get him home when he gets

here. Keep your hopes high, and send out lots of love and strength to
him and everyone down there working and waiting.

Hopeful. That's the tone she wanted to strike. There was no way,
she figured, that her strong, good-natured Sergio had been taken
down by this thing. He had to be somewhere. They just didn't know
where.

But a week went by and hundreds of posters were taped onto
streetlights, fences, and subway station walls all over the five bor-
oughs, and still there was no sign of him. The news reports were
grim—there had been many survivors and many dead, but very few
injured. Tanya continued to hold on to hope, continued to send out
optimistic emails. On September 17, Tanya wrote:

So here it is, another day, and though it really is hard to face each
new one, we are all hanging in there—it's all that we can do for Sergio
and the others. I am trying to look at it as another day closer to finding him.

And then another week went by. The news reports grew even
more grim—the rescue crews were finding very few people still
alive. The scene was more accurately described as a recovery effort.
"Hope in the beginning feels like such a violation of the loss," memoirist Gail Caldwell writes, "and yet without it we couldn't survive."
On October 2, Tanya wrote:

Today I cleaned my floors, put on some good music, opened the windows and welcomed the beautiful sunny day here. I will finish this e-mail, do some laundry, and take care of paperwork for the store. Then perhaps I'll take a walk in the garden, throw on Oprah or a good video, or just take a long nap. And all the while, as has been the case for the past three weeks, I will wait for news, and believe it or not, I am still hoping for a miracle . . .

She heard that someone had once been trapped in the rubble of an earthquake, alive, for twenty-eight days. The number twenty-eight stuck in her mind. She clung with a fierce desperation to the possibility that Sergio could be alive. "Twenty-eight days," she told people. "It's happened before. It could happen again."

Yet as the twenty-eighth day was approaching, her hope was running out. She felt like she was going crazy. "Did Sergio and I even exist?" she wondered, sleep deprived and in shock.

Then, as soon as she doubted their love, she would see some sign that confirmed it. Sergio and Tanya had always had a thing for bunnies. They sent each other cards with bunnies on them, called each other bunny, even referred to their impending postwedding bliss as the "bunnymoon." In the weeks that she waited for Sergio to come home, she saw bunnies everywhere—on the side of a truck, bustling through Jackson Heights, on a candy wrapper, on a magic show on television.

What, Tanya wondered, was the meaning of these synchronous moments? Were these real signs that Sergio was alive somewhere and just needed to be found and brought home? Or was he communicating from another realm?

On the twenty-sixth day, she couldn't stand it anymore. She decided that she had to call a psychic in Florida that a friend had told her about, a woman named Elaine, who was supposed to have a direct line to the spiritual realm beyond. Tanya remembered the discussion she'd had with Sergio about channeling—so many years ago in that messy, blissful bed—as she dialed Elaine's number on the evening of October 7.

After a quick introduction—nothing more than names, niceties, and Tanya's birth date—Elaine launched in: "You are being stripped of everything you know, so that you can come into your own power." Then she paused, her voice dropped, and she said softly, "Oh dear. You've lost someone. Your soul mate." The last stubborn bit of hope left Tanya's body with her next exhalation.

. . .

Though it had been nearly a year since Sergio's death, Tanya still held on to his favorite cereal: Honey Bunches of Oats. She felt great comfort in touching the box, knowing that Sergio's hands had once touched it as well. She knew it was crazy, but she was too sad to care much about crazy. She says, "One of my fears is that, as time passes, I'm going to forget. And then I go to my boxes. I saved everything."

It wasn't just the cereal boxes. It was the chocolate drawer (Sergio had a real sweet tooth). And the clothes. Sometimes Tanya would stand at the closet and gently finger Sergio's soccer jerseys, thinking of how much he loved the sport and when she would scream "Goal!" Even his bric-a-brac—old receipts, batteries, and loose coins—became sacred talismans to Tanya. She would rub each item and wonder when he'd set it aside. It amazed her that these things, which had once seemed so mundane, were now sources of longing for her, sacred almost. If only she could see him empty out his pockets one more time, his big hands diving in and coming out with a strange little assortment of things. That one silly action would be so wildly comforting.

Yet he would never do that again. He would never wash his hands with his favorite sandalwood soap or whistle through his teeth. He would never eat another slice of pizza at Old Palermos or make a glass of his signature "Sergio Sangria"—red wine with Fresca. He would never get his hair cut at Jimmy the Greek's. He would never refer to himself in the third person. Worst of all, he would never touch her again. "I just want him to come home," Tanya said. "I feel like life is so fake."

The outside world was jarring. People wanted to make small talk about the weather. Tanya was expected to go grocery shopping and do her laundry and keep the store running. Sometimes it made her feel like screaming, as Al Pacino so famously had in *Scent of a Woman*, "I'm in the dark here!" All that was authentic to her, internally, was lost and yet the world went on, bustling along with its Pollyanna brightness, expecting her to live as if living wasn't a dangerous and sad thing to do. The incongruence made her feel alienated from other people and numb to the world.

Even a trip to France with her mother, a vacation she'd once dreamed of, left her feeling empty. Looking out over the fields of dancing lavender, a sight she had anticipated all her life, she experienced nothing, as if her heart were responding with a blank buzz to something so beautiful.

Perhaps even worse than the blank buzz was the gut shot of envy. One of Sergio's old cop buddies called with elation in his voice and told her that he'd had a son and named him after Sergio. Tanya tried to sound joyful in her response, but the words stuck in her throat. *She* would never have a baby with Sergio. She would never hear him call someone, his big hazel eyes wide with disbelief and joy, and tell them that he was a daddy. She admits, "It's so yucky, the feelings of envy and self-pity."

These are the kinds of feelings that she is able to share with her support group of widows, knowing they will understand. She doesn't want to sound bitter or ungenerous. But when girlfriends hold their lefts hands out to her, revealing the promise of "till death do us part" sparkling on their fingers, she has to repress the sharp pang of injustice and say, "How exciting!" as if she means it, as if she could possibly mean it when her own love story was cut short.

It was Herculean just to mourn Sergio, just to come to terms with the loss of such a gorgeous bear of a man, her "Big Daddy," her true love. But she also had to mourn their future together. As Carmella B'Hahn, author of *Mourning Has Broken*, explains, "Our stories of how life might unfold, although invisible, are often as powerful and real to us as the actual present moment . . . the more vivid our imaginings of the future, the greater the loss will be felt."

Tanya reflects, "What I lost was tremendous. It wasn't just losing the love of my life. It was losing my expectations, my dreams, my future, what I thought would be my future."

Tanya remembers a dusk stroll with Sergio in their neighborhood in Queens. They spotted an old couple, wrinkled hands intertwined, and Sergio leaned over to her and said, "That's going to be you and me one day, babe."

Remembering this moment is deeply painful, like a broken promise. Pulitzer Prize–winning novelist Marilynne Robinson writes:

There is so little to remember of anyone—an anecdote, a conversation at table. But every memory is turned over and over again, every word, however chance, written in the heart in the hope that memory will fulfill itself, and become flesh, and that the wanderers will find a way home, and the perished, whose lack we always feel, will step through the door finally and stroke our hair with dreaming, habitual fondness, not having meant to keep us waiting long.

Tanya treasures the little signs she gets from beyond, the small ways in which she feels like Sergio is reaching back, reassuring her that he is still with her, but she also finds them cruel. She explains, "At moments when I'm really having a lot of despair, I feel that it's such a blessing that I can get these things, but at the same time, it's like 'Why can't you just come home?' Instead of conjuring up bunnies, conjure up flesh and bone and come home."

Sergio will not come home. He can't. The finality of it is enough to make Tanya long for her own end. "What keeps me going right now," she explains, in late 2002, "is remembering him, of course, and remembering that I am capable of a tremendous amount of love and joy . . . and guilt." Tanya pauses and dives down to the depths of her own suffering, then continues: "Guilt keeps me here. All of my friends and family keep me here. Because, believe me, sometimes the pain is so much that I don't want to be."

. . .

New York is simply too full of triggers—every little thing in the apartment, the never-ending mail about recovery logistics and therapeutic opportunities from city agencies, Sergio's favorite corner store, the skyline's altered state. Tanya feels as if the city is conspiring to keep her in the dark.

So she escapes. Or more accurately, she returns to the place where she and Sergio first fell in love. Tanya buys an apartment in Miami in October of 2002. It is a place of only happy, buoyant memories, and otherwise, a sort of comforting anonymity. In New York, Tanya is the widow. In Miami, she can be the biker chick, the new age mystic, the beautiful, mysterious woman at the bar.

• • •

The bike gives her a healing outlet. Tanya explains: "I go to Miami and get on my motorcycle. It's euphoric. There's something about sunshine, wind in the hair, road, just vastness, nature, trees, that I find soothing. You go into such a zone. You become kind of one with the road. You let everything go. Free."

Tanya's not just liberated when on her bike; she's a badass: "I feel strong when I'm on the bike, like I'm the shit. I got this 468-pound machine and I'm controlling it." At a time when the sadness makes her feel weak and vulnerable, getting on the bike brings her back to her own undeniable strength.

As early as 2003, Tanya admits, "I have this fantasy that I'm going to get this whole new life someday." She says this almost as if she were wishing to fly with her own two arms as wings, as if it is both a delicious and preposterous idea to her. Sergio, after all, was the love of her life. After losing him, there was a time when she felt as if she had lost her own one-and-only possible future, lost the opportunity to ever have a family, lost the capacity to love ever again. But the longer she is in Miami, riding her bike fast on the highways overlooking the ocean, meeting people who have never known her as Sergio's girl, letting time and quiet oxidize some of her acute pain away, she begins to let the possibility of a new life creep in.

One of the silver linings, however inadequate, of losing Sergio was a financial cushion. Though Tanya continued to run her store,

Inner Peace, returning to Queens and all its triggers at least every couple of weeks, she was no longer totally dependent on the store revenue because of the money she received from the September 11th Victim Compensation Fund following Sergio's death.

While the money helps Tanya make ends meet, she also spots an opportunity to finally give back to her mother, Eileen. Her mom adopted her, raised her and her three children while working two jobs, took care of her sick husband until his death, as well as taking care of friends and neighbors, and never complained. In 2004 and 2005, Tanya spends a lot of time and energy on purchasing and remodeling an apartment for Eileen, just ten blocks away from her own, in Miami. She makes sure that every last detail reflects her mother's tastes, needs, and unspoken desires.

It is an all-consuming project, taking her mind away from her mourning for hours at a time, providing her with the healing sensation of giving back rather than being stuck in her own funk. It's not that Tanya is done mourning, but that she is learning how to take breaks from it. Tanya describes this dynamic: "There's the half of me that's like I have to connect [to my grief], I have to be in it, but at the same time, I don't want to overwhelm myself. I want to be connected, but not to the point where it's choking me. I need to divert. I need to decompress."

Tanya's instinctual wisdom is mirrored in scientific research. Dr. George Bonanno, who has studied thousands of people in mourning, writes, "It is that respite from the trench of sadness that makes grief bearable. It is the marvelous human capacity to squeeze in brief moments of happiness and joy that allows us to see that we may once again begin moving forward."

Moving back and forth between Miami and New York isn't easy. Each time that Tanya returns to her and Sergio's apartment in Queens, she is confronted with a mountain of mail pertaining to 9/11, voice mail messages, all of the little logistics of the store. The reality of her loss sometimes stuns her all over again, the minute she walks through that apartment door.

She is essentially living a double life, but she gives herself permission. She knows that she needs it. When things get hard, she tells herself, "That chapter is finished, at least for this lifetime. Stay open. It will come. Get on your bike. Get through the days. Do what you have to do."

. . .

Tanya rolls into a gas station on "Big Daddy" with her friend Debbie clinging to her back. They spot a group of guys on souped-up motorcycles. These guys are the real deal and Debbie jumps at the chance to spark a conversation: "It's hot, right? Two girls on a bike."

The two groups end up chatting for a bit. Tanya mentions wanting to repaint the tank of her bike to honor her lost fiancé. She feels awkward inserting Sergio into conversations like these, but also obligated. The guilt she feels is ever present, particularly on days like these when she is deliberately leaving her widow identity behind and just trying to have some fun. She is comforted when she notices that one handsome guy's Harley Deuce has a firefighter-angel emblem on his license plate. *He probably gets it,* she thinks.

The girls decide to join the guys as they ride toward Fort Lauderdale. It is a carefree day, just the kind that gives Tanya great relief. But eventually it's time to head home. The looker on the Harley Deuce, who Tanya learns is named Ray, offers to ride south with her.

Once they make it home, Tanya accepts Ray's invitation for lunch along Miami Beach's Lincoln Road. She has already started dating, but she struggles with how to talk with new guys about who she is and what she has experienced. Though Tanya's support group ended in 2004, the women all stay in touch and often discuss the difficulty of simply introducing themselves when meeting new people. With Ray, it all just comes pouring out. He responds with palpable empathy: "I can tell that you really loved him."

The simplicity of it is stunning. "I did," Tanya replies. "I really did."

. . .

Having been through her own season of suffering, Tanya notices that she is able to connect more deeply to the suffering of others. "Losing Sergio was *the* experience that was my reality call," she explains. "We all have this assumption: You do good things, good things happen. That's how we're all conditioned to live until the rug gets taken out from under you and you realize, wow, there's pain in life."

Tanya has come to understand that pain is nondiscriminating, that the nearly unbearable level of loss she's weathered is not unique. Philosopher Judith Butler writes, "To grieve . . . is not to be resigned to inaction, but it may be understood as the slow process by which we develop a point of identification with suffering itself."

"Why me?" Tanya asks, but then follows: "Why not me? What makes me so special that I shouldn't be going through this? If this is for my soul's growth, let me try to be as productive as I can be."

In 2005, she decides to take a trip to South America, during which she spends a transformative week volunteering at the village of San Pedro de Casta in the Andes. The poor village lies near the ancient Inca ruins of Marcahuasi, four hours from the city of Lima. The secluded farming community that Tanya finds there holds deep ties to the once flourishing empire, and yet now the villagers struggle to get basic necessities like running water and proper housing with ventilation. Tanya is shocked to learn about the high infant mortality rate, due mostly to carbon monoxide poisoning. She doesn't hesitate to get her hands dirty to help.

Marcahuasi, a mysterious site in Peru peppered with hundreds of gigantic stone sculptures, is believed by many to be one of the world's most spiritual places, and Tanya, ever open, feels a deep connection to the people and the land there. She teaches English to the village children.

Faced with the undeniable extent of the village children's hardship, Tanya realized that she had been living life with blinders on, preoccupied with wedding planning, and inventory for the store, and soccer games. She and Sergio had been happy-go-lucky. They were also, Tanya realizes, sometimes disconnected to the misfortune of others: "I don't ever want to get to the point where I am that oblivious to the world as I was before September 11th. This is what pain is, and people encounter this everywhere."

. . .

Roman Catholic monk Thomas Merton observed, "There is in all visible things . . . a hidden wholeness." Tanya stood atop Machu Picchu, looking out at the breathtaking vista before her, and felt that hidden wholeness for the first time in years. It was her thirty-seventh birthday and she'd grown tired of the divided life. She'd come to Peru in search of some kind of wisdom about how to move forward, how to fuse her cleaved worlds together, and here, at eight thousand feet up, she'd actually gotten something like an answer.

It started as she was hiking up. She was sucking wind, really struggling to keep up with the rest of the tour group, and decided to call on her guardian angel. *Big Daddy, I need a sign that I can actually do this!* Just minutes later, a porter passed her wearing a Boca Juniors soccer jersey, the uniform of Sergio's beloved Argentinean soccer team. Tanya knew that he was with her.

As discussed earlier, psychologists historically pathologized when a person has a continued relationship with a dead loved one, but many contemporary experts in grief and healing actually see it as an adaptive, and potentially healthy, behavior. Bonanno himself admits to speaking to his dead father in an elevator. He writes, "Continuing bonds are more adaptive in a context where they are understood and culturally supported."

In other words, talking to the dead might get one committed to an asylum in the United States but might be perfectly acceptable in Bangalore. It was fitting that Tanya was communicating with her long-lost Sergio in Peru, as the Incan people are believed to have had elaborate rituals of conversing with and honoring the dead. Spanish invaders recorded detailed accounts of opulently dressed mummies being offered the finest food and drink at ceremonies.

But Sergio was not the only man communicating with Tanya that day. When Tanya finally made it to the top of the "lost city of the Incans," she reached into her backpack, as promised, and pulled out a card that Ray had written her.

Things with Ray started at a slow simmer. They would ride together on occasion, talk about everything under the sun during lunches at roadside cafés. Ray had been through a painful divorce, so he had his own scars. They talked about the pain of loss, the end of their innocence, shared fears about risking a chance for happiness again. They were good at being friends. At first, Tanya didn't see the potential for love. Her feelings for Sergio had been so all consuming, so unmistakable, so charged. With Ray, it was subtle and comforting and good. At first, she didn't recognize what was happening: "I had envisioned that the person I was going to wind up with was going to be so completely outgoing like Sergio, but Ray has this very quiet confidence about him. He didn't fit into my image of who I was going to be with."

Tanya even tried to set him up with one of her girlfriends, but Ray slowly, patiently made his way into her heart, her home, and eventually her future. Ray's card read: "I hope that while you are there, and you see this civilization that has outlasted even the dream of the builder, that you would consider building a dream with me." Ray, a former firefighter who now worked in construction, was asking her to consider a future with him.

Perhaps it was the vastness of the landscape, or maybe the strength she felt from conquering such a massive mountain despite her struggles, that led Tanya to feel so expansive. She felt as if she had the capacity to carry on her many identities—the motherless baby, the seeker, the widow, the business owner, the biker chick, and the mystic. That day in Machu Picchu, she felt as if she had the capacity to move forward: "I felt connected. Connected to Sergio, connected to the earth, connected to history. I considered my future. I'm ready to fall in love. I can't worry what other people are going to think about the person. If I'm in love with someone, that's it."

...

Tanya and Ray lay in bed, talking about Tanya's transformative trip. It was hard to explain—the level of deprivation and tenderness in the Andean village, the porter's message from beyond, the freeing vista, but Ray was a patient and curious listener. At a pause in their conversation, he leaned over and slipped an engagement ring on her finger. "I love you, Tanya," he said. "I want to marry you."

Tanya felt her epiphany atop the mountain suddenly replaced by a rush of fear. "I miss my other ring," she exclaimed without pre-meditation.

"Put it on," Ray said, reassuring her. "I would never take that away from you. One of the reasons I love you so much is how devoted you've been to Sergio. I feel like Sergio gave me a gift in you." Once again, Ray was able to quiet Tanya's fears. Through his own unshakable security, he was able to reassure Tanya that loving him didn't diminish her love for Sergio in any way.

Eventually, she understood that she was not replacing Sergio with Ray, but adding another great man into her life story: "I will be Ray's wife. I was also Sergio's fiancée. I was also my parents' daughter. I'm starting to allow myself to be comfortable in that. You bring everything forward with you."

In part, Tanya's resistance to moving on was a product of fear. She worried about experiencing the same kind of pain again—giving over her heart and her hope only to have it demolished. "How am I going to create a whole new life without being afraid it's going to be taken away?" she asked. It's a fair question for someone who has already lost so much. In fact, it's a fair question for any of us, and one frequently asked. How can we love with all of our hearts, throw ourselves into a shared life, when we know it can be taken away in an instant?

We do it because it is part of the human story, because it is what people have done for millennia, what we will continue to do. We lose. We heal. We fall in love. We create new stories, new lives out of great tragedy. We continue to take the lovely, dumb leap of faith into loving again because it's what makes our lives worthwhile; it's what makes humanity somewhat miraculous—our capacity to recover and revise and carry on.

Tanya promised to marry Ray. "I'm surrendering," Tanya explains. "I'm surrendering to the possibility that I can have a life again. Ray deserves this. He's so good."

But wholeness would not come so easily. Tanya acknowledges that she is still in process: "Integrating is painful, difficult, challenging. I had to let go of the person I became after 9/11, to let go of my widowhood. That was somebody I'd grown accustomed to being."

And it was somebody that Sergio's mother, whom Tanya had remained very close to, was accustomed to her being. Tanya understood that while she had the luxury of healing and moving forward, finding another love, Sergio's mother could never find another son. Both of them had suffered an irreplaceable loss, but Tanya's allowed for new beginnings. Delia, Sergio's mother, had to process an abrupt and unalterable end.

When Tanya finally got the nerve to break the news to Delia, that she was officially engaged to be married to someone else, Delia was honest and supportive: "I'm not ready to meet him quite yet," she told Tanya, "but I will be. I just want you to be happy."

And happy she was. On May 22, 2006, Tanya and Ray rode a big, beautiful motorcycle to a luscious outlook in Maui, looked out over the ocean, and made their new beginning official. "'From this day forward' was so significant," Tanya explains. "This is the journey. We're starting it here."

Reverend Al, a rotund local in traditional Hawaiian garb, officiated. When he rode up on his own white Harley, they knew that they were—once again—blessed from the beyond.

...

Tanya returns to New York, as always, for the anniversary of September 11th. But this time, things are undeniably different. It is a landmark five years since she lost Sergio. She is now wrapping up some of the many ongoing memorial projects that she has been so committed to over the years: a slide show of Sergio and a memorial book featuring snapshots, inspirational quotations, and people's memories of him. She will read his name in the ceremony that year.

Tanya had been diligent over the years to make sure that Sergio's name was included in any 9/11 memorial, even going so far as having a street named after him. Each year, she creates a sign honoring his memory and takes it down to Ground Zero, where she joins the other families. She describes her loyalty to this ritual and her commitment to memorializing Sergio in many ways: "I don't want people to forget that there were people, lives, dreams, loves, that were just so senselessly taken. What I can be responsible for is my story, Sergio's story. I can make sure that he's not forgotten."

But five years out, she recognizes that these rituals might need to adjust to her new, integrated life now that she's married to Ray.

She's happy to have done so many projects—both for herself and for her and Sergio's community of friends and family—to make sure that he is memorialized, but she has realized that his legacy will now live on in less explicit ways. She wonders, "Maybe by next year I'll have a baby. I don't want to feel guilty about not getting this stuff done before then. I want to go into the next chapter feeling like I did it all. Hopefully, this weekend I'll be done, and can say, 'Wow, in these five years I've done a lot for him.'"

A few weeks later, when the doctors tell her that the official start date of her pregnancy was September 11, 2006, she smiles to herself. Of course.

When Delia hears the news, she tells Tanya that she is ready to meet Ray. "I want to be a part of the baby's life," she tells Tanya. Delia flies down to Miami to visit and they arrange to meet at a restaurant. The first words out of Ray's mouth are "Hi, Mom!" Once again, Ray has managed to disarm Tanya, and now her dear Delia, with his openness and comfort in his own skin. From then on the conversation flows. When it is all over, Delia exclaims, *"¡Ya está!"* ("It's done!" in Spanish), and tells Tanya to make sure that there is always a room available for Grandma to stay over.

• • •

Emilia Grace is born the following June, her first name a tribute to Tanya's late father, Emilio. Tanya is reminded of her favorite quotation in Sergio's memorial book: "When you were born, you cried, and the world rejoiced. Live your life in such a way so that when you die, the world cries and you rejoice."

The feeling of first laying eyes on her daughter comes with its own surprise for Tanya: "I thought I would be more overwhelmed with tears, but I felt deeply calm."

Emilia Grace grows into a chubby, happy toddler—a constant reminder of the innocent goodness of hard-fought new beginnings. Samantha Rae follows a year later—due on September 11, 2008, born a week early. Both beautiful girls are manifestations of C. S. Lewis's beautiful words: "Miracles are a retelling in small letters of the very same story which is written across the whole world in letters too large for some of us to see."

The births of her children are chances for rebirth for Tanya. At first she wonders, "How do I explain Sergio to them? What would be the best, least confusing way? I think I'll just say, 'Now he's Mommy's guardian angel, and Daddy's guardian angel, and your guardian angel.'"

Tanya doesn't ride her motorcycle anymore. With two little girls at home, she's too busy, and even with her guardian angel, she's a bit more wary of the danger of that four-hundred-pound machine. She wants to be around for her daughters and for sweet Ray. Plus, she doesn't need that balm of the ride like she used to. She still has her moments of grief, without a doubt, but they are private and brief. Sergio will always be a part of her.

Tanya has been working on her own memoir, committed to

sharing her journey in hopes that it helps others who are faced with moving beyond great and so often unexpected loss. She reflects, "I don't think I ever thought that I would get to this point where I would merge to this degree. I always thought that it would be two separate things. But I am so content and so proud that I have been able to bring it all together."

Conclusion

So what have we to learn from these often sad, quietly triumphant stories?

Well, for starters, we have learned that much of what we thought was true of grief is simply wrong. Kübler-Ross, albeit well intentioned, was wrong. Freud was wrong too. Kübler-Ross, while a pioneer in the field, failed to highlight the individualized process by which mourners grieve. Freud's writing, albeit different from his own experience, renders mourning as a linear experience that reaches an end. Grief is not a linear, tidy, or tamable experience. When people are led to believe it is, they are left feeling inadequate and sometimes guilty. Grief doesn't really end, so much as reconstitute itself. As Pulitzer Prize–winning writer Gail Caldwell wisely observes, "We never get over great losses; we absorb them."

Counter to our quintessential American industriousness, grief cannot be crossed off a to-do list. As soon as you think you've successfully "completed" it, that you are done with mourning, the feeling sneaks up on you in the quiet hours of night or in the middle of the grocery aisle. You are undone once again. And sometimes very, very pissed off at being strapped with sadness when you thought you'd "done everything right" to rid yourself of it.

Grief also can't be conquered, wrestled to the ground by a strong, determined spirit. It's simply bigger than you, no matter how big you might fancy yourself to be. To fight grief is to throw oneself, with naive audacity, against the fattest Buddha in the world, sitting and meditating, unmoved by your desperate flailing. He won't be done until he's done, just as grief won't leave your heart until it's ready to be absorbed into your emotional bloodstream.

Or perhaps it never really leaves. When writer Meghan O'Rourke and psychologist Leeat Granek created a research survey on grief on Slate.com last spring, they were shocked to find that within just a couple of weeks nearly 8,000 people had responded. A large portion (33 percent) said that they experienced their loss more than eight years ago, suggesting that even if you adapt, it is still a huge part of your new life. Twenty-seven percent said that they never went back to feeling like themselves or "normal" after their loss.

Grief changes you. Plain and simple. It alters the way in which you understand yourself, your community, and the world around you. It creates a whole new dimension to love—that which you've felt, that which you will feel. It deepens and widens your understanding of suffering, not just as it alchemizes in your own idiosyncratic psyche and body, but as it emerges for others. Your sadness becomes the world's sadness, and also its potential for transformation. Elie Wiesel, who survived incomprehensible hardship during the Holocaust, explains it this way: "Because I remember, I despair. Because I remember, I have the duty to reject despair."

We remember our suffering—a state that, indeed, is twinned with despair—and yet, in the act of remembering and honoring what we've experienced, we turn away from despair. Once you have known the pain of excruciating, incomprehensible loss, you can't un-know it. You know it forevermore, for yourself, but also in empathy for the rest of humanity who must revel and suffer through this universal experience of birth and death, life constantly in flux, decaying and renewing, coming and going. It is one of those great paradoxes of the human condition—when you endure suffering, you also earn the empathy that is born of surviving it and the beauty of its acute end.

Grief is not obedient and it's not finite. In this way, it's actually quite like love. We love people until we must grieve them, two sides of the same universal coin. In the throes of love, we easily forget that either death or grief will follow. This is good. Even necessary. It keeps us brave.

After all, how could Tanya have ever thrown herself so wholeheartedly into her life with Sergio if she'd known that it would one day end, abrupt as a slammed door? How could Nick have had any normalcy in his relationship with his mom if he'd known that one day, out of nowhere, she would be wrenched from his young life, leaving a gaping hole? How could Larry have ever built his entire life around the unconditional love he discovered with Gene if he had known that conditions outside of his control would one day rob him of a future with his beloved? None of us know what heartbreak we might bear, nor should we. Love is a risk you take despite all the evidence that it might one day crush you.

You can't avoid it—the loving and the losing—but the consolation is this: Your love never actually has to end. This is what these stories teach us. Accidents, disease, natural disasters, terrorists, or innocent old age might take away the man you love, your mother or mentor, your dear, sweet brother, but it can never kill your precious knowing of that person. Flesh and bone are cremated, buried, decomposed, but memories are immaterial and eternal. You have no choice about death, but you have the power to keep your sacred relationship alive.

While letting go, as Freud asserted, is an essential part of the grieving process, the healthiest mourners are those who also carry on. The courageous survivors contained within this book accept the physical deaths of their loved ones and carry their memories and their special relationships on in various, very personal ways. Freud was primarily interested in the negative aspects of being attached to the deceased, while we discovered the transcendent possibilities of staying intertwined. Far from damaging the subjects, the ongoing process of integrating their lost loved ones—their values, gifts, memories—into their future strengthens and enlivens them, even adding meaning to their lives.

Brian is still honoring his brother each and every day, not just through his continued commitment to Ground Zero, but through his unfettered commitment to his family. When he lights up a room talking about "my girls," he's really talking about both his two daughters and Michael's. Nick is working on an online start-up for social good called TwoSeed. It's innovative platform combines the brain of business acumen with the heart of altruism, just as his mom always did in her work, friendships, and family. Tim will devote himself, until his last breath, to serving the memories of his fallen brothers—whether that's through his own website, with advocacy work, or mentoring the next generation. In this way, Terry and his other heroic friends are never truly gone from his daily life.

Interestingly enough, even Freud himself admitted that it wasn't really possible to strike dead—completely "finish" mourning—those we love the most. When his daughter Sophie Halberstadt died from influenza in 1920, he was devastated and found that he wasn't so much "working through" the pain of his child's death as learning to coexist with its profundity. In 1929, writing to his friend Ludwig Binswanger, whose son had recently died, he explained:

> *My daughter who died would have been thirty-six years old today. . . . Although we know that after such a loss the acute state of mourning will subside, we also know we shall remain inconsolable and will never find a substitute. No matter what may fill the gap, even if it be filled completely, it nevertheless remains something else. And actually this is how it should be. It is the only way of perpetuating that love which we do not want to relinquish.*

Many of us, like Freud, find ourselves stripped bare through the grief process. We would like to think that we can mourn in alignment with some comforting timeline that promises eventual resolution. We would like to think that our theories will keep us protected from the messiness of it all. We would like to think that we can control the process. But everyone, eventually, is humbled by the universal human experience of loving and losing. Each of us is unique in the way we manage those feelings and live on with the love.

The way in which resilience ebbs and flows in these eight stories is no more linear than grief. Though researchers have made a lot of progress since resilience was first introduced into scientific literature in the early '70s, there is still no fixed or absolute idea about what it is, exactly, and perhaps even more important for our everyday lives, how to develop it. DNA, self-confidence, communication skills, and the capacity to make realistic plans and manage strong feelings are all thought to influence how resilient we are when faced with difficult times, but most of these capacities and skills are difficult to measure.

One thing is certain—the most resilient people are those with supportive relationships. We see this over and over in the stories that have unfolded in the previous pages. It is the unconditional love of caring family and friends that buoys all of these survivors in their rockiest moments. It's also their capacity to reach out for support when they need it and to accept help that allows them to flourish. Nick speaks so often about the comfort of being surrounded by his family and close friends throughout the years. Tanya tears up when she talks about "the girls"—her support group of widows who understood her grief as no one else could. Tim finds refuge in his brother's company—a safe place to talk about his dark feelings over a light beer. We have so little control in this life, to be sure, but one thing we can do to protect ourselves is to create sturdy and loving relationships in our lives. There's no question that these bonds are the glue that keeps us from truly falling apart in times of trauma and loss.

The commitment to help others in their time of need following the events of September 11th, of course, was the source of so much inspiration and so much physical and mental suffering, as well. For those who experienced that day and its aftermath firsthand, there was the sudden and stunning death of a different kind: the death of a former self. The person who walked on the hollowed disaster of Ground Zero on September 12, 2001, was the not the same one who walked anywhere on September 10, 2001. Brian, Charles, Joe, Tim—each of them was forever altered by what they saw there. Debbie, though farther afield of the actual carnage, would never be the same after knowing that the country's consciousness had grown brittle in the face of it. She had to make her way in a world where her deepest values and her heritage were newly suspect.

There were times when it seemed that these brave survivors tried their old identities on, only to find that they no longer fit, or tried to bully a new story, a more hopeful story, out of the sadness. As they metabolized their pain, as they processed their memories, as they considered the "why" of their own survival among so many who were lost, they navigated their way into new narratives. It turns out that just as we can't hurry the grieving process along, recovery from trauma has its own unpredictable timing as well. One's soul is rebuilt, not according to a schedule, but according to a mystery. It is psyche and breath, memory and vulnerability, muscle and lung, coordinating to create a new kind of living.

Bishop Stephen T. Bouman writes about his mission with the traumatized immediately following September 11th in his book, *Grace All Around Us: Embracing God's Promise in Tragedy and Loss*: "In the weeks after I would visit each of the eighteen conferences of our synod with only one agenda: how is your soul?" Secondary trauma, like that experienced by so many on and in the days following September 11th, is, in a sense, a clarifying force for the soul. By strapping on his boots and walking straight down to Ground Zero that autumn morning, Charles strengthened his own sense of himself as a helper, a server, and a soul mate, of sorts, to those in need. Joe, likewise, rose to the challenge of the most morbid of roles following the death and destruction in his dear city, and in so doing, performed his final brave act as one of New York's finest; his soul settled down to grandchildren and rest thereafter. Brian, in his unwavering days of "filling one bucket" at a time, allowed his own soul the salve of feeling useful; when he stopped feeling useful, of course, the grief rushed in.

Brian, like so many, staved off the real sadness with the numb of constant activity—not just a phenomenon of post-traumatic stress, of course, but of the contemporary human condition. We make ourselves so busy, so plugged in, preoccupied, and self-important that we often forget just how vulnerable we really are. Erikson, writing of disaster and its brutal lessons, observes, "People are encouraged to think that they can control the best in nature and the worst in themselves, and they continue to think so until the momentum of some adventure carries them beyond the limits of their own intelligence or stamina." Disaster and death trim the fat off of our lives in an instant, leaving behind only what is most precious—our health, our families, our sense of purpose.

The surprise is that there is great release in the humbling that coincides with grief and recovery. Pema Chödrön writes, "As human beings, not only do we seek resolution, but we also feel that we deserve resolution. However, not only do we not deserve resolution, we suffer from resolution. We don't deserve resolution; we deserve something better than that. We deserve our birthright, which is the middle way, an open state of mind that can relax with paradox and ambiguity."

The texture of the stories that these eight survivors offer us is testament to this birthright. In each of their losses, and each of their unique and quite beautiful journeys to process and integrate those losses, we see the best of the human spirit. We see Delia embracing the man who would give the woman who was to be her daughter-in-law, Tanya, a second chance at joy. We see Larry being buoyed by the God that others told him hated his way of loving. We see Nick acknowledging that his mother is, perhaps, more complex than he allowed, and so, in turn, is his way of honoring her. Tim's loss of so many metaphorical brothers brings him even closer to his biological brother.

These decade-long stories of restoration are rife with paradox. Though Debbie's whole life is constructed around building bridges, her own path explodes in her face; though her mission is to facilitate dialogue between cultures, her own words are lost in the media's sensational translation. Charles's commitment to promoting the health of others destroys his own. Ground Zero has become both the bane of Brian's existence and his deepest joy and honor. Joe lives with death in his past and his mind, and birth in his present and his heart.

It has been ten long years for each of these eight survivors, ten long years for all of us, truth be told. We experienced anthrax; the war in Afghanistan; Enron's bankruptcy; No Child Left Behind; the birth of Homeland Security; the Iraq War; the conclusion of the Human Genome Project; the invention of Facebook, Wikipedia, Google, and Twitter; conflicts in Darfur, the Middle East, and Liberia; Abu Ghraib; earthquakes, tsunamis, hurricanes, and heat waves; the reelection of George W. Bush; the Kyoto Protocol; Avian flu; H1N1; Harry Potter; the election of Barack Obama; Deepwater Horizon; terrorists attacks; mining disasters; spacecraft launches; *American Idol*; and solar eclipses.

As overwhelming as this partial list is, it's only the public record— the kind of stuff that gets debated in the nation's op-ed pages and makes it into history books. The private stories are equally important and often unheard or neglected. In these ten years, we have, indeed, fought wars, weathered natural disasters, seen unprecedented technological, political, and cultural shifts. We have also cried and laughed, cooked and celebrated, mourned and danced, prayed and accepted. We have come to understand the modern life as one riddled with unpredictable public events that threaten our private lives, and yet persevered in the face of fears and vulnerability. We have loved one another well, and known that this is—in the end—what it's really all about.

In these ten long, healing years, there have been many formal moments marking the recovery from the tragic events of September 11th—the first and every annual commemoration, breaking ground for the Freedom Tower, the 9/11 Commission Report, the Tribute in Light etc.—but there have also been so many unmarked moments, the kind that simply accumulate in a life intentionally and bravely lived. Debbie watched as her sweet son got married. Joe walked his granddaughter to school. Larry sat side by side with his fellow congregants. Tim walked by the water. Nick had dinner with his dad. Charles slapped his domino down. Tanya rode her motorcycle into the sunset.

These, too, were remarkable acts, experiences worth recording and savoring. But the way history gets written often leaves out the small but meaningful moments—the caring gestures, the euphoric yelps, the one-foot-in-front-of-the-other reality of rediscovering joy after a long season of sadness. As Frederick Buechner writes, "Listen to your life. See it for the fathomless mystery it is. In the bored and pain of it, no less than in the excitement and gladness; touch, taste, smell your way to the holy and hidden heart of it, because in the last analysis all moments are key moments, and life itself is grace."

None of their journeys has really ended. For the purpose of writing about a critical decade of loss and renewal, we imposed the essential elements of any story—beginning, middle, and end. But the truth is that all of these scarred and brave human beings are still becoming, still integrating their losses, still writing their stories. As are we all.

Acknowledgments

We would like to thank all of the talented people who are part of the Project Rebirth family, especially Brian Rafferty, for being our shepherd through this process, and Caitlin Olson, for serving as the center of so many spokes. Frank Moretti, none of this would have existed without you. Our deepest gratitude goes to Jim Whitaker, who had the rare mix of sensitivity, audacity, and determination necessary to see his dream through to the end.

We would also like to thank the team of people who worked behind the scenes to make this book a reality, starting with our agents, Richard Pine and Tracy Brown. Thank you for your commitment to our careers and our voices. We are grateful that Amy Hertz initially believed in us and this book, and that Mike Frankfurt and Mark Merriman stepped forward to shape the collaboration. Thank you also to Michael Preston for the terrific technological assistance.

Our hats off to all of the creative and committed people at Dutton, starting with our fierce editor, Carrie Thornton. Carrie, your capacity to see the form within the stone made all the difference. A huge thank you is also in order for Stephanie Hitchcock for her tireless work near the end. Your commitment, communication, and editorial help in the final months were indispensible. Thank you to the entire publicity team, who does the critical work of making sure that all these words and good intentions actually get to the readers.

We also want to thank all the people who generously gave of their time to talk to us about their own experiences and share their important thoughts about the events of September 11th, grief, trauma, and recovery: George Bonanno, Jeff Kleinberg, Emanuel Shapiro, Katherine Shear, Ada Dolch, Michael Kessler, Marc Brackett, Rabbi Michael Paley, Father Kevin O'Brien, Mary Dluhy, John Dluhy, Albert Brok, Mary Marshall Clark, Josh Gordon, Leeat Granek, Linda Meisler Berko, Cheri Lovre, Sheila Brown, (the late) Roz Winter, Margaret Micle, Naomi Wolf, Mark Wilding, April Naturale, Wendy Jager Hyman, Helen Churko, Carole Saltz, Gardner Dunhan, Wendy Flammia, Judith Logue, and Craig Richards. Deep gratitude to Lester Lenoff for your keen insight and ready psychoanalytic translations.

For their indispensable research, we thank Krystie Yandoli, Julie Morris, Barbara Weber Floyd, Adam Klein, and Katherine Scharf. We would also like to toast the incisive and steady Andres Richner, who swooped in with a fresh perspective and an investigative eye at exactly the moment we needed him. You are our superhero. Thank you to Courtney's writers group for all of the support, particularly Kimmi Auerbach for her counsel in the toughest moments and Jennifer Gandin Le for her beautiful rendering of love in post–September 11th Brooklyn. Thank you to Robin's colleagues at the Inner Resilience Project—especially Linda Lantieri, Carmella B'Hahn, Martha Eddy, Lynne Hurdle-Price, Ixchel Allblood and Cynthia Smith Miler—for their support of this project and for holding the space for educators to renew themselves since September 11, 2001.

We give thanks for our colleagues at the Woodhull Institute for Ethical Leadership, where we met, for the ongoing support of both of us and our work. Thank you to our Star Factor community, and especially to Janet Patti, for her ongoing love and support of us. And deep gratitude goes to many colleagues and good friends—you know who you are—whose continuous conversations through the years nurtured us and kept us intellectually inspired on this topic and many others.

As always, we are deeply indebted to and grateful for our incredible families. The empathy and compassion that we brought to this project, the belief in resilience, hope, and healing, was born out of our deep love for each of you, and the love we always receive in return.

From Courtney: Thank you to my parents, Jere and Ron, and my brother, Chris. You were my first thoughts on September 11th and still are. Thanks also to Mary Austin Speaker; a first sister was never so lucky. Thank you also to John, for believing so unwaveringly in my worth, for all of the careful editing, and, of course, for the Hamptons rescue. It is unendingly strengthening to have you in my corner.

From Robin: Thank you to my husband, Frank, my rock, and to my children, Scott and Melissa—you are the lights of my life always. (You are my "forever presents"!) Thank you to my parents, Roz and Dave (who is always with us), for always believing in me. Thanks always for your lifetime of being there—and for comedic times— to my brother, Eric, and sister-in-law, Jacquie, and my nephews and niece, Justin, Daniel, and Julia. A big thank you also to my stepchildren—Kiki, Tonio, and Nicco—and to my extended family— Elaine and Artie (who is always with us), Jan and Charlie, and Billy for being there, with us, through it all—traumas, dramas, and all celebrations. And great thanks to Lena Gordon, Lisa Neal, and Santiago Enrique Michel for supporting me so that I can do my work.

At the risk of being read as self-congratulatory, we want to thank each other.

Robin, thank you for so many years of mentoring and mothering, for your inextinguishable idealism, and for your commitment to making this work, come hell or high water. I am so glad that I got up early at the Woodhull Institute for Ethical Leadership ten years ago.

Courtney, thank you for showing up early that day at Woodhull— you always do! Thank you for allowing me to be part of your incredible journey. Mentoring you has been a gift for me too. Thank you for your dedication to this project, even in the challenging times, for your commitment to excellence and your tireless work ethic, for your beautiful writing, and especially for your authenticity in our relationship,

We are most profoundly grateful to the incredible people profiled in this book: Tanya, Tim, Brian, Larry, Joe, Charles, Debbie, and Nick. Your collective courage in sharing your journeys is deeply moving and left us awestruck over and over again. You are each a testament to the strength, goodness, and resilience of the human spirit. Thank you for trusting us.

Appendix A:

Centers or Organizations Devoted to Dealing with Grief, Trauma, and First Responders

I. Internet Resources

Bereavement Services
A social network for those who have lost a loved one.
http://www.mybereavement.net

Crisis Management Institute
Addresses crisis response, technical assistance, training, and violence prevention, particularly in schools.
www.cmionline.org

Good Grief
Online resources and referrals for those grieving or wishing to support someone in grief.
www.good-grief.org

GriefNet
Online community of persons dealing with grief, death, and major loss.
www.griefnet.org

Grief's Journey

Focuses on the bereavement for the loss of a spouse and life partner. *www.griefsjourney.com*

II. National Organizations

America's Camp

One-week camp in the Berkshire Mountains of Massachusetts for children who lost a parent or sibling as a result of the attacks on September 11, and for the children or siblings of the firefighters or law enforcement officers lost in the line of duty at any time.

www.americascamp.org

Bereaved Parents of the USA

National self-help group that offers support, understanding, compassion, and hope, especially to the newly bereaved, be they bereaved parents, grandparents, or siblings struggling to rebuild their lives after the death of their children, grandchildren, or siblings.

www.bereavedparentsusa.org

Comfort Zone Camp

Weekend bereavement camp for children who have experienced the loss of a parent, sibling, or primary caregiver.

www.comfortzonecamp.org

Compassionate Friends

Self-help support organization with nearly six hundred chapters, offering friendship, understanding, and hope to families grieving the death of a child of any age, from any cause.

www.compassionatefriends.org

National Child Traumatic Stress Network

Dedicated to improving access to care, treatment, and services for traumatized children and adolescents exposed to traumatic events.

www.nctsnet.org

National First Responders Organization

Created by and for the nation's first responders—police, firefighters, medical personnel—NFRO supports first responders and their families.

www.nfro.org

National Organization of Parents of Murdered Children

Provides the ongoing emotional support needed to help parents and other survivors facilitate the reconstruction of a "new life" and to promote a healthy resolution.

www.pomc.com

Tragedy Assistance Program for Survivors

Provides support for those who have suffered the loss of a military loved one, regardless of the relationship to the deceased or the circumstance of the death.

www.taps.org

Trauma First Aide Associates

Organization of social workers, trauma therapists, nurses, and mindbody practitioners experienced in working with trauma survivors.

www.tfaassociates.com

III. Northeast

The Alcove Center for Grieving Children and Families

Provides bereavement support services for the southern New Jersey area. The Alcove provides peer support groups for children ages three to eighteen and adult groups for their surviving parent, grandparent, or guardian.

www.thealcove.org

Camp Haze

One-week summer experience for children who lost a loved one on September 11, 2001.

www.camphaze.org

Center for Grieving Children

Provides support to grieving children, teens, families, and communities in Portland, Maine, through peer support, outreach, and education.
www.cgcmaine.org

Center for Grieving Children, Teens, and Families

Offers support groups for children, ages six to eighteen, in Pennsylvania, who have experienced the death of someone close, as well as education programs for families and support and referral.
www.grievingchildren.org

Center for Loss and Renewal

Psychotherapy and consultation group located in New York City dedicated to the practice of life-transition therapy.
www.lossandrenewal.com

The Dougy Center

Provides support in a safe place where children, teens, young adults, and their families grieving a death can share their experiences.
www.dougy.org

Families of September 11

Membership organization for family members, survivors, responders, or others impacted by the terrorist attacks on September 11th.
www.familiesofseptember11.org

Family Resource and Counseling Centers

Focused on Pennsylvania, offers professional counseling services grounded in Christian principles and faith.
www.fracc.org

FealGood Foundation

Created to spread awareness about the catastrophic health effects on 9/11 first responders, and to provide assistance to these people and their families. Additionally, the organization aims to create a network of advocacy on 9/11 healthcare issues.
www.fealgoodfoundation.com/index.html

International Trauma Studies Program

New York University program that develops and shares innovative approaches to address the psychosocial needs of trauma survivors, their families, and communities.

www.itspnyc.org

The Trauma Center

Provides comprehensive services to traumatized children and adults and their families in and around Brookline, Massachusetts.

www.traumacenter.org

Tuesdays Children

Provides support for the children of 9/11 and others impacted by global terrorism.

www.tuesdayschildren.org

The World Trade Center Survivors' Network

Volunteer-run organization that employs a wide range of initiatives and activities to serve survivors of the World Trade Center attacks on September 11.

www.survivorsnet.org

IV. Midwest

Amanda the Panda

Offers children and family grief services including weekend camps in Iowa.

www.amandathepanda.org

Barr-Harris Children's Grief Center

Provides services to children in Illinois who have lost a parent through death, divorce, or abandonment.

www.barrharris.org

Camp Fire USA Central Ohio's Camp Atagahi (Grief Camp)

Camp Fire USA Central Ohio Council created Camp Atagahi, located at Wyandot, Ohio, to help children cope with the death of someone close to them.

www.centralohiocampfire.org/camp/grief-camp/

The Center for Grief, Loss and Transition

Based in St. Paul, Minnesota, provides specialized therapy and education in the areas of complicated grief, trauma, and life transition.

www.griefloss.org

Center for Grief Recovery and Therapeutic Services

Based in Chicago, Illinois, helps persons who are dealing with emotionally intense experiences such as grief, loss, trauma, depression, or abuse.

www.griefcounselor.org

Solace House

A haven for families throughout the Kansas City metropolitan area.

www.solacehouse.org

V. West

Center for Loss and Life Transition

Located in the mountains of Fort Collins, Colorado, dedicated to companioning grieving people as they mourn transitions and losses that transform their lives.

www.centerforloss.com

The Contra Costa Crisis Center

Focused on Contra Costa County, California, provides individual and group counseling to youths and adults mourning the death of a loved one.

www.crisis-center.org

FIRST Responder Support Team

Referral network of counseling providers for law enforcement personnel in the state of Texas.

www.emergencyresponderfirst.com

The Grief Recovery Institute

Provides programs and workshops throughout California for individuals dealing with loss and offers grief recovery training programs for health-care professionals in North America.

www.grief-recovery.com

H.O.P.E. Unit Foundation

Helps people in Southern California whose lives have been touched by loss by providing group support, educational programs, and information to alleviate and mitigate the burdens and aloneness of bereavement.

www.hopeunit.org

Trauma Intervention Programs of Arizona

Works to prevent secondary victimization that all too often occurs with loss-of-life incidents.

www.tipofaz.org

VI. South Central

The Amelia Center

Located in Birmingham, Alabama, specializes in family grief counseling.

www.ameliacenter.org

Child Trauma Academy

Based in Houston, Texas, offers consultation, education, and training services to assist individuals and organizations in their work with high-risk children.

www.childtrauma.org

Kidzcope

Formerly Three Trees Inc., Kidzcope is based in Wichita, Kansas, and serves children whose dreams have been destroyed by the death of a loved one by helping them find ways to cope and to heal.

http://www.kidzcope.org/

A Place That Warms the Heart

Based in Louisiana, provides support groups for adults, children, and adolescents dealing with the death of a loved one.

www.placethatwarmstheheart.fws1.com

Stars: Grief Support for Kids

Based in Crestview Hills, Kentucky, provides grief support services for children who have experienced the death of a loved one.

www.starsforchildren.com

VII. South Atlantic

Full Circle Grief Center

Based in Richmond, Virginia, provides children with creative ways to express their grief and remember their loved one.

www.fullcirclegriefcenter.org

Point of Hope Grief Counseling Center

Based in the Washington, D.C., area, provides support services following community and individual tragedies.

www.pointofhope.org

Roberta's House

Based in Baltimore City, Maryland, provides a safe and supportive community for grieving children and families through peer support, education, community awareness, and empowerment.

www.robertashouse.org

Appendix B:

Books on Grief, Loss, and Resilience

Albom, Mitch. *Tuesdays with Morrie: An Old Man, a Young Man, and Life's Greatest Lesson.* New York. Broadway. 2002.

Barbash, Tom. *On Top of the World: Cantor Fitzgerald, Howard Lutnick, and 9/11: A Story of Loss and Renewal.* New York. HarperCollins. 2003.

B'Hahn, Carmella. *Mourning Has Broken.* Bath, UK. Crucible Publishers. 2002.

Bonanno, George. *The Other Side of Sadness.* New York. Basic Books. 2009.

Borysenko, Joan Z. *It's Not the End of the World: Developing Resilience in Times of Change.* Carlsbad, CA. Hay House. 2009.

Brenner, Grant H., Daniel H. Bush, and Joshua Moses. *Creating Spiritual and Psychological Resilience: Integrating Care in Disaster Relief Work.* New York. Routledge. 2009.

Brooks, Robert, and Sam Goldstein. *Nurturing Resilience in Our Children: Answers to the Most Important Parenting Questions.* New York. McGraw-Hill. 2002.

———. *The Power of Resilience: Achieving Balance, Confidence and Personal Strength in Your Life.* New York. McGraw-Hill. 2004.

Bouman, Stephen Paul. *Grace All Around Us: Embracing God's Promise in Tragedy and Loss.* Minneapolis. Augsburg Books. 2007.

Chansky, Tamar Ellsas. *Freeing Your Child from Negative Thinking: Powerful, Practical Strategies to Build a Lifetime of Resilience, Flexibility, and Happiness.* Philadelphia. Da Capo Lifelong Books. 2008.

Chödrön, Pema. *Start Where You Are.* Boston. Shambhala Publications. 1994.

———. *When Things Fall Apart.* Boston. Shambhala Publications. 1997.

Davidson, Richard, and Daniel Goleman. *Training the Brain* (audiotape). Northampton, MA. More Than Sound Productions. 2008.

Didion, Joan. *The Year of Magical Thinking.* New York. Vintage. 2007.

Dwyer, Jim, and Kevin Flynn. *102 Minutes: The Untold Story of the Fight to Survive the Twin Towers.* New York. Times Books. 2005.

Edwards, Elizabeth. *Resilience: The New Afterword.* New York. Crown Archetype. 2009.

Emerson, David, Elizabeth Hopper, Bessel Van Der Kolk, and Peter A. Levine. *Overcoming Trauma Through Yoga: Reclaiming Your Body.* Berkeley. North Atlantic Books. 2011.

Erikson, Kai T. *Everything in its Path: Destruction of Community in the Buffalo Creek Flood.* New York. Simon & Schuster. 1976.

Fitzgerald, Helen. *The Grieving Teen: A Guide for Teenagers and Their Friends.* New York. Fireside. 2000.

Greenland, Susan Kaiser. *The Mindful Child: How to Help Your Kid Manage Stress, and Become Happier, Kinder, and More Compassionate.* New York. Free Press. 2010.

Groopman, Jerome. *The Anatomy of Hope: How People Prevail in the Face of Illness.* New York. Random House. 2004.

Herman, Judith. *Trauma and Recovery: The Aftermath of Violence—from Domestic Abuse to Political Terror.* New York. Basic Books. 1997.

Keltner, Dacher. *Born to Be Good: The Science of a Meaningful Life.* New York. W. W. Norton. 2009.

Kübler-Ross, Elisabeth. *On Death and Dying: 40th Anniversary Edition.* New York. Scribner. 1997.

Kumar, Sameet M. *Grieving Mindfully: A Compassionate and Spiritual Guide to Coping with Loss.* Oakland, CA. New Harbinger Publications. 2005.

Kushner, Rabbi Harold. *When Bad Things Happen to Good People.* New York. Anchor. 2004.

La Capra, Dominick. *Writing History, Writing Trauma.* Baltimore. Johns Hopkins University Press. 2001.

Lantieri, Linda. *Building Emotional Intelligence: Techniques to Cultivate Inner Strength in Children.* Boulder, CO. Sounds True Incorporated. 2008.

Lesser, Elizabeth. *Broken Open: How Difficult Times Can Help Us Grow.* New York. Villard Books. 2005.

Levine, Peter A. *Healing Trauma: A Pioneering Program for Restoring the Wisdom of Your Body.* Berkeley. North Atlantic Books. 2010.

Levine, Peter A., and Maggie Kline. *Trauma-Proofing Your Kids: A Parents' Guide for Instilling Confidence, Joy, and Resilience.* Berkeley. North Atlantic Books. 2008.

Levine, Peter A., and Gabor Mate. *In an Unspoken Voice: How the Body Releases Trauma and Restores Goodness.* Berkeley. North Atlantic Books. 2010.

Lewis, C. S. *A Grief Observed.* New York. Harper One. 2001.

Lipsky, Laura van Dernoot with Connie Burk. *Trauma Stewardship: An Everyday Guide to Caring for Self While Caring for Others.* San Francisco. Berrett-Koehler Publishers. 2009.

McGee, Teresa R. *Transforming Trauma: A Path Toward Wholeness.* Maryknoll, NY. Orbis Books. 2005.

Miller, Beth. *The Woman's Book of Resilience: 12 Qualities to Cultivate.* Boston. Conari Press. 2005.

Morales, Rosanna. *Empowering Your Pupils Through Role-Play: Exploring Emotions and Building Resilience.* New York. David Fulton Books. 2008.

O'Rourke, Megan. *The Long Goodbye.* New York. Riverhead. 2011.

Rando, Therese A. *How to Go On Living When Someone You Love Dies.* Lexington, MA. Bantam. 1991.

Rinpoche, Sogyal. *The Tibetan Book of Living and Dying.* Revised and updated edition. New York. Harper One. 1994.

Ripley, Amand. *Unthinkable: Who Survives When Disaster Strikes—and Why.* New York. Three Rivers Press. 2008.

Salzberg, Sharon. *A Heart as Wide as the World.* Boston. Shambhala Publications. 1997.

Seligman, Martin E.P. *The Optimistic Child: A Proven Program to Safeguard Children Against Depression and Build Lifelong Resilience.* New York. Mariner Books. 2007.

Sheehy, Gail. *Middletown America: One Town's Passage from Trauma to Hope.* New York. Random House. 2005.

Sherwood, Ben. *The Survivors Club: The Secrets and Science that Could Save Your Life.* New York. Grand Central Publishing. 2009.

Siegel, Daniel J. *Mindsight: The New Science of Personal Transformation.* New York. Random House. 2010.

Solnit, Rebecca. *A Paradise Built in Hell.* New York. Viking Adult. 2009.

Sontag, Susan. *Regarding the Pain of Others.* New York. Picador. 2003.

Teachers College Press with Maureen Grolnick, ed. *Forever After: New York City Teachers on 9/11.* New York. Teachers College Press. 2006.

Temes, Roberta. *Solace.* New York. AMACOM. 2009.

Tolle, Eckhart. *The Power of Now: A Guide to Spiritual Enlightenment.* Novato, CA: New World Library; Vancouver: Namaste Publishing. 1999.

Viorst, Judith. *Necessary Losses: The Loves, Illusions, Dependencies, and Impossible Expectations That All of Us Have to Give Up in Order to Grow.* New York. Fireside. 1986.

Walton, Charlie. *When There Are No Words.* Ventura, CA. Pathfinder Publishing. 1996.

Wicks, Robert J. *Bounce: Living the Resilient Life.* New York. Oxford University Press. 2009.

Yoder, Carolyn, and Howard Zehr. *The Little Book of Trauma Healing: When Violence Strikes and Community Is Threatened.* Intercourse, PA. Good Books. 2005.

Young, William P. *The Shack.* Newbury Park, CA. Windblown Media. 2007.

Zajonc, Arthur. *Meditation as Contemplative Inquiry: When Knowing Becomes Love.* Herndon, VA. Lindisfarne Books. 2008.

Appendix C:

Films on Grief, Loss, and Resilience

Always, Amblin Entertainment, 1989.

Coming Home: Families, Courage and Resilience, BIANYS Documentary Films, 2010.

Dearly Loved: Dealing with the Death of a Parent, Calgary Health Region Grief Support Center, 2005.

Forrest Gump, Paramount Pictures, 1994.

The Gifts of Grief, Martie Productions, 2005.

The Last Mountain, Fanlight Productions, 2004.

Like Water for Chocolate, Arau Films Internacional, 1992.

On Our Own Terms: Moyers on Dying, Bill Moyers, PBS, 2000.

Ordinary People, Paramount Pictures, 1980.

Out of Order: Dealing with the Death of a Child, Calgary Health Region Grief Support Center, 2005.

Phantom Limb, Jay Rosenblatt Films, 2005.

Pioneers of Hospice: Changing the Face of Dying, Madison Deane Initiative, 2004.

Project Rebirth, Jim Whitaker, 2011.

Star Trek Generations, Paramount Pictures, 1994.

Steel Magnolias, Rastar Films, 1989.

Strong at the Broken Places: Turning Trauma into Recovery, Cambridge Documentary Films, 1998.

Uncoupled: Dealing with the Death of a Spouse, Calgary Health Region Grief Support Center, 2006.

7/23